Pocket Rough  S0-AGL-657

HONG KONG
AND MACAU

written and researched by

DAVID LEFFMAN

Contents

INTRODUCTION TO

HONG KONG
AND MACAU

Facing each other across the Pearl River estuary, Hong Kong and Macau offer an exciting yet easy entry into the Chinese world. Colonies of Britain and Portugal respectively until they were returned to mainland China in the 1990s as Special Administrative Regions (SARs), today their southern Chinese heritage is increasingly apparent. Among the hi-tech infrastructure and the population's Westernized outlook, conservative traditions persist, from shrines to the god of wealth and age-old festivals, to the way contemporary architectural design takes principles such as *feng shui* into account. Former colonial ties are most obvious in the fact that many people speak English as well as Cantonese, and in Macau's decidedly un-Chinese antique buildings.

WALKWAY IN CENTRAL, HONG KONG ISLAND

Best places for a stunning view

Hong Kong's premier lookout points are The Peak (p.39) and the Tsim Sha Tsui waterfront (p.64), between the Star Ferry terminal and Avenue of Stars – both dazzling after dark, when the whole harbourside area lights up like a Christmas tree. In Macau, head to the crenellations atop the Fortaleza do Monte (p.108), where antique cannons are aimed at the casinos lining Avenida da Amizade.

Hong Kong's famously futuristic harbourside architecture has long set the standard for similar cityscapes rearing up all over Asia. There's also a broad mix of other architectural styles here, encompassing Mong Kok's ramshackle town housing, traditional clan villages in the New Territories, Tai O's stilt-houses and the centuries-old temples which are dotted around. The accompanying markets and street life are compellingly frenetic, while the shopping – though no longer a bargain – offers the chance to compare a vast range of products sold everywhere from open-air stalls to hi-tech malls. Hong Kong is also one of the best places in the world to eat Cantonese food, while the territory's Western influence means there's a plentiful selection of bars and nightspots.

Surprisingly, Hong Kong's outlying areas remain fairly undeveloped, with a countryside of beaches, rugged hills, wild coastline and islands – although none of it especially remote – where you can escape the pace and claustrophobia of the downtown areas. Hong Kong's only real downside is that the overwhelming commercialism and consumption make it hard to engage with the underlying Chinese culture – though you can glimpse it at Happy Valley's horse races, Mong Kok's Bird Market or simply by watching early-morning tai chi practitioners going through their routines in Kowloon Park. Cultural barriers also drop at the several annual Chinese festivals sprinkling the calendar – Chinese New Year, the Dragon Boat Races and Cheung Chau Bun Festival are the liveliest – when even visitors will find it hard not to get caught up in the action.

Smaller and more visually attractive than its neighbour, Macau is also ethnically Chinese, but its charms rest more on its backdrop of old Portuguese churches, forts and streets, which lend the place a colonial-tropical ambiance. Its tiny scale means you can see just about everything on an easy day-trip from Hong Kong, while its superb food marries Portuguese, Chinese, Goan, Brazilian and African influences, washed down with Portuguese port and brandy. As far as the Chinese are concerned, however, Macau's main appeal is in its many casinos – it's the only place on Chinese territory where they are legal – which draw in swarms of punters from Hong Kong and mainland China.

When to visit

Hong Kong and Macau are **tropical**, which means generally humid conditions throughout the year. From December to February is the coolest period (16ºC), though usually dry; temperatures rise from March through to May (23ºC) and rainfall increases; while from June until September the weather is steaming hot (30ºC), often with fearsome **typhoons** (from the Chinese *tai fung* – "big wind"), whose storms affect sea traffic. Tourist levels are even year-round, but book accommodation in advance, especially for international sporting events and for Chinese New Year in January or February.

GRAND LISBOA CASINO, MACAU

HONG KONG AND MACAU AT A GLANCE

>> EATING

In Hong Kong, the downtown areas – Hong Kong Island's north shore between **Sheung Wan** and **Causeway Bay**, and the Kowloon peninsula opposite, including **Tsim Sha Tsui**, **Jordan** and **Mong Kok** – are absolutely jammed with restaurants. These cover all budgets and, along with native Cantonese cooking, quite a range of international cuisines. In Macau the bias is towards Portuguese and indigenous Macanese dishes, with restaurants thickest around **Largo do Senado**, though don't overlook village locations at **Taipa** and **Coloane**. Wherever you eat, expect brusque service, little elbow room and a hot and noisy atmosphere, just how the Chinese like it.

>> DRINKING

Macau has no real drinking culture, but Hong Kong's bar scene focuses on **Lan Kwai Fong** in Central, where dozens of lively bars and pubs compete for the swarms of yuppies, office workers, expats and tourists that descend nightly. It's not hard to find somewhere to fit your mood, be it sports bar, Irish pub or quiet terrace. Serious drinkers – mostly expats – gravitate east to seedier **Wan Chai**, while across the harbour in **Tsim Sha Tsui** you'll find a thin scattering of Brit-style pubs. Bars open from late afternoon through to the early hours; drinks are pricey, so look out for happy hours.

>> SHOPPING

Thanks to the wonders of internet shopping, the affordable electronics gear Hong Kong was once so famous for is no longer a particularly good deal, though you will be able to lay your hands on just about every model and brand of computer, camera, mobile phone and MP3 player yet invented at specialist warehouses in **Wan Chai**, **Mong Kok** and **Sham Shui Po**. Jewellery shops are everywhere in **Central**, **Tsim Sha Tsui** and **Mong Kok**, and the same goes for clothing, with various bargains available in Mong Kok, Sham Shui Po and on **Ap Lei Chau** island. If you're looking to shop for antiques, head to the dozens of galleries strung along **Hollywood Road**.

>> NIGHTLIFE

Clubs in Hong Kong fire up after about 9pm, though as most are located in the city's bars, you can often get drinks before the music kicks off. Expect DJs or house bands playing mainstream rock through to punk and jazz; **Lan Kwai Fong**'s bars lend themselves to more intimate events, with larger clubs and dance floors in **Wan Chai** and Tsim Sha Tsui's **Knutsford Terrace**. Hong Kong doesn't see many big international acts, though Cantopop and Mandopop stars – from Hong Kong, China and Taiwan – play at the **Hong Kong Coliseum** or **Queen Elizabeth Stadium**.

OUR RECOMMENDATIONS FOR WHERE TO EAT, DRINK AND SHOP ARE LISTED AT THE END OF EACH CHAPTER.

Day One in Hong Kong

1 Victoria Park > p.50. Begin the day watching tai chi practitioners performing their slow-motion shadow-boxing routines in downtown Hong Kong's largest public space.

2 Times Square > p.51. This is what Hong Kong is all about: cruising fashion boutiques in huge, multilevel malls.

3 Queen's Road East > p.49. A kilometre of quirky shops and the unusual Pak Tai and Hung Shing temples – not to mention ghostly Nam Koo Terrace.

4 Hong Kong Park > p.38. Attractive landscaped hillside right above busy Queensway; spot colourful tropical birds inside the walk-through Edward Youde Aviary.

Lunch > p.45. Drop into the *Lok Cha Tea House* at the K.C. Lo Gallery, for vegetarian *dim sum*.

5 Bank of China tower > p.35. This knife-shaped tower is a major player in the *feng shui* wars being waged in Hong Kong's competitive financial district.

6 Hollywood Road > p.40. Antique stores, curio shops and art galleries surround the smoky Man Mo Temple, dedicated to the twin gods of war and culture.

7 Sheung Wan Market > p.41. A wholesale market for dried medicinal herbs, seafood and animal products.

Dinner >p.46. Time for a Cantonese blowout on roast goose at *Yung Kee* restaurant in Central, before hitting Lan Kwai Fong for a nightcap.

Day Two in Hong Kong

1 Kam Tin > p.85. Old walled clan village, famous for resisting the British takeover of the New Territories in 1897 – at which point the iron gates were confiscated.

2 Wishing Trees > p.92. Hong Kong's folk beliefs are on display at these two fig trees, where people write wishes on strips of red paper and attach them to notice boards.

3 Hong Kong Wetland Park > p.86. Bird hides, a butterfly garden and an excellent aquarium provide a fun insight into the Chinese take on the natural world.

Lunch > There aren't many restaurants in this part of the New Territories, so pack a picnic and make use of the outdoor tables in Hong Kong Wetland Park.

4 Mong Kok markets > p.78. Head back to town and mix with the crowds searching for bargains, or a pet, at Mong Kok's Goldfish and Ladies' markets.

5 Temple Street Night Market > p.75. Souvenirs, alfresco dining, fortune-telling and Cantonese opera – this market is more like street theatre.

Dinner > p.75. Hong Kong offers great seafood, so knuckle down with the locals at Temple Street Night Market's outdoor tables, and feast on chilli crab, steamed shellfish and fresh grilled snapper.

6 Kowloon waterfront > p.64 & 67. Get a spectacular view of one of the world's greatest cityscapes, all lit up in a riot of competing neon.

Old Macau

Old Macau's Portuguese-influenced cathedrals, forts and cobbled lanes make a complete break from the hi-tech, modern towers dominating Hong Kong's harbour, and Macau's newer casino district along Avenida da Amizade.

1 Largo do Senado > p.106. Old Macau's main square, sided in pastel-coloured religous institutions and arcaded shops.

2 São Paulo facade > p.107. Landmark frontage of a seventeenth-century cathedral, all that remains after a devastating fire in 1835.

3 Fortaleza do Monte > p.108. There are great views from this seventeenth-century fort, complete with old cannons and a museum outlining Macau's lively history.

4 Leal Senado > p.106. Browse the art gallery and decorative Portuguese tiling inside Macau's one-time seat of government.

Lunch > p.121. Lunch on coffee and *nata*, Portuguese custard tarts, at the *Ou Mun Café*.

5 Rua da Felicidade > p.114. Macau's former red-light district is now a busy street of hotels, restaurants and *pastelarias* selling almond biscuits and roasted meats.

6 Largo do Lilau > p.114. Picturesque residential square in the Barra, one of the first to be settled by Europeans.

7 A-Ma Temple > p.115. Site of the oldest temple in Macau, dedicated to the southern Chinese protector of sailors and fishermen.

Dinner > p.121. Dig into some of the city's finest indigenous Macanese cooking at *Litoral*, near the old harbour.

Budget Hong Kong

Hong Kong is generally considered an expensive place to visit, but there are plenty of free (or nearly free) sights and activities, if you know where to look.

1 Zoological and Botanical Gardens > p.37. Shaded city park with decorative flowers, orangutans, gibbons, lemurs and cages of birds.

2 Edward Youde Aviary > p.38. Huge walk-through aviary with balconies at canopy height, allowing close-up encounters with birdlife.

3 Views from The Peak > p.39. Pay a few dollars for the bus – or walk up if you feel like more of a challenge – and The Peak offers superlative vistas over this dynamic city.

Lunch > p.46. *Tsui Wah* is a budget Hong Kong institution: three floors of trademark fishball soups, Hainan chicken rice and fried noodles.

4 Viewing Bay, Central Plaza > p.48. Head to Wan Chai's Central Plaza, Floor 46, during office hours for superb free views of the harbour and Peak.

5 Star Ferry > p.48. Pay a pittance to enjoy one of the world's most iconic views: Victoria Harbour seen from the water.

6 Kowloon Park martial arts performances > p.69. Martial artists demonstrate their prowess every Sunday afternoon; the shows finish with colourful lion dances.

7 Mong Kok Goldfish Market > p.78. Probably the most offbeat of Hong Kong's traditional street markets, where these lucky fish are traded in quantity.

Dinner > p.83. Queue up to eat at the world's cheapest Michelin-star rated restaurant, *Tim Ho Wan* – best for *dim sum*-style dumplings and savoury pastries.

Big sights

1 Tian Tan Big Buddha See religion writ large at this huge bronze statue, which sits serenely between Lantau's peaks and the Po Lin Monastery. > **p.98**

2 View from The Peak
Almost all of Hong Kong is visible from Victoria Peak, with a staggering view north across the harbour, Kowloon and into the New Territories. > **p.39**

3 São Paulo facade
Macau's most famous colonial Portuguese building, though only the intricately carved stonework shell remains after a fire in 1835. > **p.107**

4 Star Ferry This evocative ride across Victoria Harbour allows water-level views of shipping activity, framed by row upon row of Central's hi-tech towers. > **p.30**

5 Harbour at night Central's futuristic skyline is one of the world's great cityscapes – catch the Symphony of Lights at night. > **p.67**

Festivals

1 **Mid-Autumn Festival** Cakes stuffed with sweet bean paste are eaten all over Hong Kong to celebrate both the harvest and a fourteenth-century uprising by the Chinese against their Mongol overlords. > **p.141**

2 Fireworks at Chinese New Year Hong Kong and Macau usher in the Chinese New Year with brilliantly intense firework displays – Hong Kong's in particular is like spending forty minutes in the middle of a war zone. **> p.140**

3 Tai Hang Fire Dragon Forty metres of smoking, glowing dragon, studded with incense sticks, is paraded through this Hong Kong Island suburb after dark during the Mid-Autumn Festival. Come prepared for the crowds. **> p.141**

4 Tai Chiu Bun Festival A week-long extravaganza on Cheung Chau island (in April or May), featuring outdoor Chinese theatre, dragon dances, stilt-walking and 20m-high towers made of steamed buns. **> p.140**

5 Dragon Boat Races A Chinese tradition dating back over two thousand years, when teams of narrow-hulled, dragon-headed boats race to commemorate the drowning of the famous statesman Chu Yuen in the third century BC. **> p.141**

Museums

1 **History Museum** Fun recreation of Hong Kong's past, with whole streets reconstructed amid the usual glass cases of historical artefacts. **> p.68**

2 Science Museum A great place to take children on a wet day, with heaps of exhibits to prod, poke and dismantle – they might even accidentally learn something about physics. > **p.68**

3 Museum of Coastal Defence Nineteenth-century British complex of gun emplacements and underground tunnels protecting the eastern end of Hong Kong harbour, now a display of military history. > **p.53**

4 Museum of Art An engaging introduction to traditional Chinese painting, calligraphy, pottery and metalworking, with rotating exhibitions of contemporary art. > **p.66**

5 Museu Marítimo Lively museum in Macau, with scores of lovingly built scale models of wooden fishing vessels. > **p.115**

Dining

1 Roasted meats Cantonese cooking excels in roasted goose, pigeon and pork, the latter served thinly sliced or incorporated into buns or pastries. Best experienced at a *yum cha* session or at specialist restaurants like *Yung Kee*. > **p.46**

2 Macanese food Restaurants such as *Litoral* provide mammoth portions of Macau's unique dishes, including "African Chicken" and *feijoada* (bean and sausage stew). **> p.121**

3 Alfresco seafood Head to Lei Yue Mun in Kowloon, or Lamma and Cheung Chau islands, for the freshest in Cantonese seafood, cooked the way you want it, straight from the tank. **> p.82 & 105**

5 Wonton noodle soup Everyone in Hong Kong has a favourite hole-in-the-wall serving this classic Hong Kong snack of ravioli-like *wonton* with noodles in soup – you won't go wrong at *Tsim Chai Kee*. **> p.46**

4 Yum cha Sample this classic Cantonese meal (also known as *dim sum*) at a teahouse, where a host of small sweet and savoury dumplings are accompanied by a pot of fragrant tea. A good bet is the *Luk Yu Tea House*. **> p.45**

Urban pursuits

1 Shopping Electronics, gold, precious stones, antiques, clothing and pirated gear – Hong Kong has vast shopping malls to meet your needs whatever your budget. > **p.42, 54 & 82**

2 Lan Kwai Fong Unwind over a drink or two at the heart of Hong Kong's club and bar scene – a score of riotous dens provide booze and music until the small hours. > **p.36**

3 Casinos Spend an evening on a crawl around a handful of Macau's lively gaming halls, ranging from the glitzy to the decidedly downmarket. > **p.116, 117 & 119**

4 Horseracing Join the crowds of eager, hard-bitten punters for a night at Hong Kong's weekly horse races at the aptly named Happy Valley Racecourse. > **p.52**

5 Tai chi Head to green spaces such as Victoria Park in the early morning to see mostly elderly practitioners going through their slow tai chi routines, said to maintain health and flexibility. > **p.50**

Outdoor trips

1 **Picnic at Bride's Pool** Pleasant, popular woodland picnic area with waterfalls and streams, easily reached by bus from Tai Po market via the hamlet of Tai Mei Tuk. > **p.93**

2 Pink-dolphin spotting Take a boat out to look for these rare creatures, of which only sixty survive in the waters around Hong Kong. **> p.101**

3 Ocean Park Hong Kong's first theme park, complete with pandas, marine aquarium and terrifying roller coaster. **> p.58**

4 Tai Long Wan beach Probably the longest, most secluded strip of sand in all Hong Kong, though getting here from Sai Kung town requires a little pre-planning. **> p.94**

5 Dragon's Back hike An easy introduction to Hong Kong's outdoor attractions, on this two-hour hike over a wild headland down to an attractive beach. **> p.61**

BEST OF HONG KONG AND MACAU

Markets

1 Jade Market Watch serious buyers weigh up tiny slivers of this green gold – or buy a souvenir piece for yourself. > **p.75**

3 Goldfish, bird and flower markets Hong Kong's three most traditional markets, surprising to find in such an outwardly modern city. > **p.78**

2 Temple Street Fun, touristy night market, good for a souvenir, an alfresco meal or even an impromptu performance of Cantonese opera. > **p.75**

4 Three Lamps District Macau's answer to Hong Kong's Sham Shui Po – copious fruit and veg, plus clothing stalls with cut-price rates and an eccentric range of sizes and fittings. > **p.112**

5 Sham Shui Po Ramshackle run of budget haberdashery and discounted clothing stores, with an interesting flea market in nearby Ap Liu Street. > **p.78**

PLACES

Hong Kong Island: Central and around

Set on Hong Kong Island's north shore, Central and the adjoining districts are where the city coalesced after Hong Kong was seized by the British in 1841. Businesses blossomed between Victoria Harbour and The Peak's steep lower slopes, a narrow strip with so little room that buildings had no choice but to evolve upwards into a forest of tall concrete and glass towers interconnected by a web of elevated walkways. Central's atmosphere is contemporary and upmarket: banks all have their headquarters here, shopping opportunities are high-end, and it throngs with clubs, bars and restaurants. For a contrast, seek out older buildings or unwind in Hong Kong Park, while a trip up The Peak offers superlative views of the city and a real break from the crush at street level.

THE STAR FERRY

Ⓜ Central/Tsim Sha Tsui. Daily 6.30am–11.30pm, every 6–12min. Lower deck $2, air-conditioned upper deck $2.50. MAP P.32–33, POCKET MAP G4

By far the best way to arrive in Central is by Star Ferry over from Tsim Sha Tsui, dodging container ships and coastal vessels along the way. The sight of Central's skyscrapers, framed by the hills and looming up as the ferry makes its seven-minute crossing of busy Victoria Harbour, is one of the most thrilling images of Hong Kong, especially when the buildings are lit up after dark. The portly vessels, each named *Evening Star*, *Northern Star* etc, have been running since 1898, and the current 1950s-style green-and-cream livery together with wooden decks and seating are charmingly anachronistic. This isn't just a tourist sight though – the double-decker boats carry about one hundred thousand passengers a day, mostly locals, so come prepared for crowds.

VIEW ACROSS VICTORIA HARBOUR TO THE ISLAND

Victoria Harbour

Central is the best place to ponder Hong Kong's magnificent **Victoria Harbour**, from whose Cantonese label (*Heung Gang* or Fragrant Harbour) the entire SAR takes its name. This safe haven for shipping was what drew the British to the island in the first place, and after the colony became established, international trading concerns – which at the time depended entirely on maritime transport – were naturally attracted here. Today, Hong Kong's money-making enterprises have shifted into Central's towers, and the harbour is shrinking as land is reclaimed in order to build still more skyscrapers: at 1km across, the harbour is half as wide as in 1840. This narrowing has reduced the harbour's ability to flush itself clean and, with some five million people living around the harbour, its water is dangerously polluted – though long-promised sewage treatment plants have yet to be built.

Despite this, it's still difficult to beat the thrill of crossing the harbour by boat; alternatively, you can walk along Central's landscaped waterfront or Tsim Sha Tsui's Avenue of Stars for a view of the maritime activity that originally made Hong Kong great – junks, ferries, motorboats, container ships, cruise liners and sailing boats all pass through. Twenty thousand ocean-going ships sail via the harbour every year, and thousands of smaller boats depart from here on their way to the Pearl River estuary and China.

IFC2 AND EXCHANGE SQUARE

Connaught Rd and Finance St Ⓜ Central, Exit F. MAP P.32–33, POCKET MAP E5/D5

Just west of the Star Ferry Pier is the **International Finance Centre**, a business and shopping complex overlooking the Outer Islands Ferry Piers. The **IFC Mall** is one of the smartest and busiest in Central and the complex's **IFC2 Tower** reaches 420m high – even higher than the Peak Tram's upper terminus – and was Hong Kong's tallest building until the ICC tower in West Kowloon opened in 2010. Home to the Hong Kong Monetary Authority, IFC2's 88 floors are so well proportioned that its height is disguised until you consciously measure it against adjacent structures, or see its upper storeys hidden by cloud. Sadly, the tower is closed to the public.

Inland from the International Finance Centre are the three pastel-pink, marble and glass towers of Hong Kong's **Stock Exchange**, sprouting from Swiss architect Remo Riva's **Exchange Square**. The adjacent piazza has sculptures by Henry Moore and Elizabeth Frink, while the interior is entirely computer-operated: the buildings' environment is electronically controlled, and the brokers whisk between floors in state-of-the-art talking elevators.

STAR FERRY SERVICE

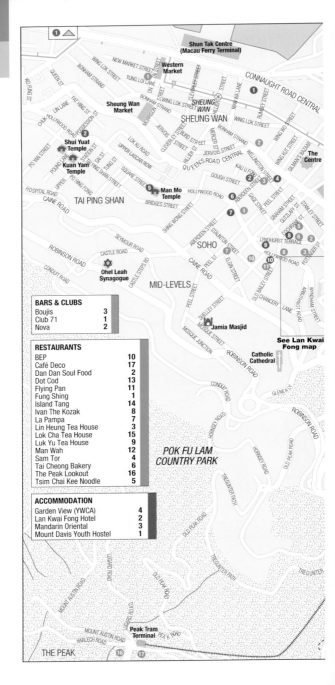

BARS & CLUBS

Boujis	3
Club 71	1
Nova	2

RESTAURANTS

BEP	10
Café Deco	17
Dan Dan Soul Food	2
Dot Cod	13
Flying Pan	11
Fung Shing	1
Island Tang	14
Ivan The Kozak	8
La Pampa	7
Lin Heung Tea House	3
Lok Cha Tea House	15
Luk Yu Tea House	9
Man Wah	12
Sam Tor	4
Tai Cheong Bakery	6
The Peak Lookout	16
Tsim Chai Kee Noodle	5

ACCOMMODATION

Garden View (YWCA)	4
Lan Kwai Fong Hotel	2
Mandarin Oriental	3
Mount Davis Youth Hostel	1

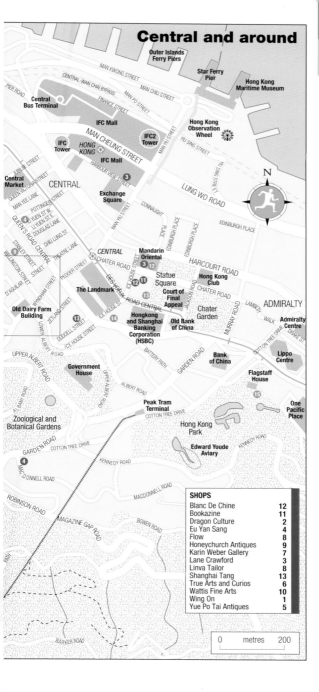

Central and around

Outer Islands
Ferry Piers

Star Ferry
Pier

Hong Kong
Maritime Museum

MAN KWONG STREET

CENTRAL-WAN CHAI BYPASS

MAN CHIU STREET

PIER ROAD

Central
Bus Terminal

FINANCE STREET

MAN PO STREET

IFC Mall

Hong Kong
Observation
Wheel

MAN CHEUNG STREET

IFC2
Tower

IFC
Tower

HONG
KONG

IFC Mall

HARBOUR VIEW STREET

MAN YU STREET

YU SING STREET

Central
Market

CENTRAL

Exchange
Square

3

LUNG WO ROAD

N

QUEEN VICTORIA STREET

QUEEN'S ROAD CENTRAL

MAN YEE LANE

POTTINGER STREET

LI YUEN ST W.

LI YUEN ST E.

DOUGLAS LANE

CONNAUGHT

CHIU LUNG ST.

EDINBURGH PLACE

MAN YU STREET

STANLEY STREET

THEATRE LANE

EDINBURGH PLACE

EDINBURGH PLACE

WELLINGTON STREET

CENTRAL

CHATER ROAD

Mandarin
Oriental

3 12

HARCOURT ROAD

D'AGUILAR STREET

PEDDER STREET

Statue
Square

Hong Kong
Club

CHATER ROAD

WYNDHAM STREET

The Landmark

DES VŒUX ROAD CENTRAL

12 11

Court of
Final
Appeal

JACKSON ROAD

ADMIRALTY

Old Dairy Farm
Building

ICE HOUSE ST.

13

Chater
Garden

MURRAY ROAD

LAMBETH WALK

COTTON TREE DRIVE

WALK

DRAKE ST.

Admiralty
Centre

ZETLAND STREET

DUDDELL STREET

14

Hongkong
and Shanghai
Banking
Corporation
(HSBC)

Old Bank
of China

Lippo
Centre

UPPER ALBERT ROAD

13

ICE HOUSE STREET

BATTERY PATH

GARDEN ROAD

Bank
of China

Government
House

UPPER ALBERT ROAD

ALBERT ROAD

Flagstaff
House

15

One
Pacific
Place

TAI WAI PATH

Peak Tram
Terminal

COTTON TREE DRIVE

KENNEDY ROAD

Zoological and
Botanical Gardens

GARDEN ROAD

COTTON TREE DRIVE

Hong Kong
Park

Edward Youde
Aviary

4

M.G. O'DONNELL ROAD

KENNEDY ROAD

ROBINSON ROAD

MACDONNELL ROAD

MAGAZINE GAP ROAD

BOWEN ROAD

MACDONNELL ROAD

PEAK RD

ROBINSON ROAD

BARKER ROAD

SHOPS	
Blanc De Chine	12
Bookazine	11
Dragon Culture	2
Eu Yan Sang	4
Flow	8
Honeychurch Antiques	9
Karin Weber Gallery	7
Lane Crawford	3
Linva Tailor	8
Shanghai Tang	13
True Arts and Curios	6
Wattis Fine Arts	10
Wing On	1
Yue Po Tai Antiques	5

0   metres   200

STATUE SQUARE

Ⓜ Central, Exit K. MAP P.32–33, POCKET MAP E6

The pedestrian underpass from the Star Ferry concourse emerges into Statue Square, heart of the late-nineteenth-century colony, though now uncomfortably bisected by Chater Road. The northern segment is bounded to the east by the members-only **Hong Kong Club**, housed inside a modern, bow-fronted tower; this is faced by the **Mandarin Oriental Hotel**, which hides an opulent interior inside a dull, box-like casing.

Across Chater Road, the southern half of Statue Square was once full of sculptures of the colony's founders and leaders, though only one remains: that of **Sir Thomas Jackson**, a nineteenth-century manager of the Hongkong and Shanghai Bank. This area is a meeting point for the territory's two hundred thousand Filipina *amahs*, or maids, who descend en masse on Central each Sunday to sociably picnic, shop, read, sing and have their hair cut. Filipinos comprise the largest non-Chinese population in Hong Kong, alongside minority groups of European, Indian and Pakistani descent.

The impressive, colonial-style granite structure with dome and colonnades on Statue Square's eastern side is the former Supreme Court, built in 1898, which until 2013 housed **LEGCO**, Hong Kong's

governing Legislative Council. This was Hong Kong's nearest equivalent to a parliamentary building, but after the council relocated east along the harbour, the building reverted to its previous function, and today houses the Court of Final Appeal.

THREE BANKS

Ⓜ Central, Exit K. MAP P.32–33, POCKET MAP E6–E7

Crossing the southern half of Statue Square and the busy Des Voeux Road puts you right underneath Sir Norman Foster's **Hongkong and Shanghai Banking Corporation (HSBC)** headquarters, which opened in 1986. The whole battleship-grey building is supported on eight groups of giant pillars and it's possible to

Elevated walkways

Many of the buildings in and around Central are linked together by a web of elevated walkways, a useful escape from the overwhelming crowds at street level – if you can navigate your way through connecting buildings. Using these it's just about possible to walk between Sheung Wan, Central, the Star Ferry Terminal and Wan Chai without touching the ground.

Feng shui

Whatever the scale of a building project, the Chinese consider divination using **feng shui** (literally "wind and water") an essential part of the initial preparations. Reflecting Taoist cosmology, *feng shui* assesses how buildings must be positioned so as not to disturb the spiritual attributes of the surrounding landscape, which in a city naturally includes other buildings. Structures must be favourably orientated according to points on the compass and protected from local "unlucky directions" (features that drain or block the flow of good fortune) by other buildings, walls, hills, mountain ranges or water. It's not difficult to spot smaller manifestations of *feng shui* around buildings in Hong Kong, such as mirrors hung above doors or woks placed outside windows to deflect bad influences. Water features create positive *feng shui* (it is believed that wealth is borne along by the water), hence the price of harbour-view real estate.

walk right under the bank and come out on the other side – a necessity stipulated by the *feng shui* belief that the old centre of power on the island, Government House, should be accessible in a straight line by foot from the Star Ferry. You look up through the glass underbelly into a 60m-high atrium, with floors suspended from coathanger-like structures and linked by long escalators that ride through each storey, and open offices ranged around the central atrium. The public banking facilities are on the first two floors, so you can ride the first couple of escalators from street level to have a look. The bronze lions at the front, named **Stephen** and **Stitt** after former HSBC directors, date back to the 1930s – one is still scarred from World War II shrapnel.

Across Garden Road to the east, I.M. Pei's 315m-high **Bank of China** is an angular, dark-glass building which towers over the HSBC building by 145m, its sharp edges designed to metaphorically "cut" into its nearby rival in a demonstration of aggressive *feng shui* (see box, above). Similarly, the BOC's knife-like

profile stabs skywards like a *feng shui* antenna, to draw down good luck from the heavens before any can reach its shorter competitors. A viewing platform on Floor 43 is open during office hours – bring your passport to gain access.

Next to the HSBC, the **Old Bank of China** still stands, a diminutive but solid stone structure dating from 1950, which looks like a fossilized ancestor of its modern incarnation. It's now occupied by the **China Club**, a wealthy, members-only haven.

FENG SHUI COMPASS

QUEEN'S ROAD AND DES VOEUX ROAD

Ⓜ Central, Exits B, C & D. MAP P.32-33, POCKET MAP A4-D6

Queen's Road has been Central's main street since the 1840s, when, prior to land reclamation, it was on the waterfront. Running south from it, just west of HSBC, Duddell Street is home to **Shanghai Tang** (see p.43), one of Hong Kong's most recognisable brands, featuring designer clothing that blends traditional Chinese hems with pop art colours and designs.

Parallel to Duddell Street, **Ice House Street** was named after a building that once stored blocks of imported ice for use in the colony's early hospitals; following it uphill brings you onto Lower Albert Road, where the early twentieth-century **Old Dairy Farm Building**, in brown-and-cream brick, today houses the *Fringe Club* (see p.47) and the Foreign Correspondents' Club, a retreat for journalists, diplomats and lawyers.

Running west, Queen's Road and parallel **Des Voeux Road** (with its tramway) take in some of the territory's most exclusive shops and malls. These include **The Landmark** shopping complex, on the corner of Pedder Street and Des Voeux Road, which boasts a fountain in its atrium and is a key hub in the **pedestrian walkway** system that links all of Central's major buildings.

Whether you follow Queen's Road or Des Voeux Road west from here, look out for the parallel alleys which run between the two, **Li Yuen Street East** and **Li Yuen Street West**; both are packed tight with stalls selling women's clothes, silkwear, children's clothes, fabrics, imitation

handbags and accessories. Southwest of these alleys, over Queen's Road, **Pottinger Street**'s steps are similarly clogged with stalls selling ribbons, flowers, locks and other minor items.

Just west of Central Market, at 99 Queen's Road Central, is **The Centre**, designed by architect Denis Lau, and by night one of the most eye-catching features of the island's skyline. The building's horizontal bars of light change colour constantly and perform a dancing light show nightly at 8pm, best seen from The Peak or the Kowloon waterfront.

LAN KWAI FONG

Ⓜ Central, Exit D. MAP P.37, POCKET MAP D6

The network of streets south of Queen's Road contains a burgeoning array of trendy pubs, bars, restaurants and clubs, at the heart of which is a sloping L-shaped lane whose name, Lan Kwai Fong, is now used to refer to the whole area. The entertainment kicks off mid-afternoon, with many places remaining open until dawn. Lan Kwai Fong is mostly frequented by expats and Chinese yuppies – a good district to meet young, aspiring locals.

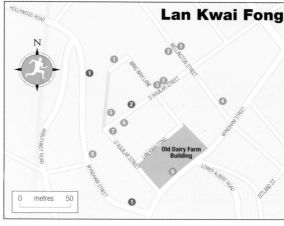

Lan Kwai Fong

BARS & CLUBS		Insomnia	7	RESTAURANTS	
Bit Point	5	Keg	6	Tsui Wah	1
D26	3	Le Jardin	1	Yung Kee	2
Fringe Club	9	Magnum Club	4		
Havana Bar	2	Origin	8		

SHOPS		ACCOMMODATION	
Margaret Court Tailoress	2	Hotel LKF	1
Teresa Coleman	1		

THE ZOOLOGICAL AND BOTANICAL GARDENS

Entrances on Glenealy St and Albany Rd
Ⓜ Central, Exit K. Daily 6am–7pm. Free.
MAP P.32–33, POCKET MAP D7

Perching on the slopes south of Upper Albert Road, overlooking Central, are the low-key Zoological and Botanical Gardens, which opened in 1864. The **gateway and lions** at the main entrance commemorate Chinese soldiers who died defending Hong Kong in the 1940s; once inside, there's a nice mix of shrubs, trees and paved paths, with close-ups of the upper storeys of the Bank of China Tower and HSBC, but the main draw is the **aviaries**, home to rare cranes, songbirds and wildfowl. West across Albany Road (via an underpass) is a collection of primates, including lemurs, gibbons and orangutans.

GOVERNMENT HOUSE

Upper Albert Rd Ⓜ Central, Exit K. Gardens and parts of the house open annually; dates announced in the local press. Free. MAP P.32–33, POCKET MAP D7

Government House was the residence of Hong Kong's colonial governors from 1855 until the SAR's return to China in 1997. Hong Kong's current Chief Executive, CY Leung, has also taken up residence here despite the building's colonial associations and notoriously bad *feng shui* – made worse, no doubt, by the Bank of China (see p.35). The house is a strange blend of styles (the turret was added by the Japanese during World War II, when the building served as their military headquarters), and the gardens are notable for their rhododendrons, azaleas and a huge fishpond.

HONG KONG PARK

Ⓜ Admiralty, Exit C1. Daily 6am–11pm. Free. MAP P.32–33, POCKET MAP E7

South from the Bank of China across Cotton Tree Drive, Hong Kong Park is beautifully landscaped in tiers up the hillside, though tackling all the steps is tough going in hot weather. Among the trees and boulders are ornamental lakes and waterfalls stocked with turtles and pelicans, alongside which a continual procession of brides pose for wedding photographs. Specific sights include a **conservatory** with dry and humid habitats for its orchids, cacti and trees, and the superb **Edward Youde Aviary** (daily 9am–5pm; free), an enormous, walk-through mesh tent, covering a piece of semi-tropical forest, home to some eight hundred tropical birds. Despite their bright plumage, many of the resident species of parrots, waterfowl, forest pigeons and flycatchers can be surprisingly hard to spot, even with wooden walkways at branch height. A separate walkway just outside the top of the aviary passes between cages of endangered hornbills, whose massive hooked beaks were once fashioned into belt buckles by the Chinese aristocracy.

At the northern corner of Hong Kong Park is the elegantly colonial **Flagstaff House**, built in 1844 as the office and residence of the Commander of the British Forces in Hong Kong. Today, it stands in defiance of the surrounding skyscrapers, its cool white walls, shutters, high ceilings and polished wooden floors the epitome of understated colonial charm. It houses a fine collection of traditional Chinese teapots, cups and tea-making paraphernalia as the **Museum of Teaware** (daily except Tues 10am–6pm; free), documenting China's two-thousand-year love affair with tea drinking, and how the process has changed with time. You can sample different brews next door at the atmospheric **Lok Cha Tea House** (see p.45) inside the K.C. Lo Gallery, then browse the gallery's collection of seal stones – elegantly carved personal name stamps used by the Chinese in the old days to sign official documents.

THE LIPPO CENTRE

Queensway Ⓜ Admiralty, Exit B. MAP P.32–33, POCKET MAP F7

The Lippo Centre is an eye-catching, segmented structure of mirrored glass designed by American architect Paul Rudolph for Australian millionaire Allan Bond in 1998. Supported on huge grey pillars, interlocking steel and glass spurs trace their way up the centre's twin hexagonal towers, creating an unmistakable landmark – though there's nothing of interest inside.

LIPPO CENTRE

VIEW FROM THE PEAK

THE PEAK

MAP P.32–33, POCKET MAP B9

The wooded, 552m heights of The Peak – officially Victoria Peak – give you the only perspective that matters in Hong Kong: downwards, over Central and the magnificent harbour. Property up here, always favoured for being an escape from the high summer temperatures at sea level, has become the astronomically expensive prerogative of the colony's elite: residents include politicians, bank CEOs, various consul-generals and assorted celebrities.

The best way to ascend is aboard the **Peak Tram** (daily 7am–midnight, every 10–15min; $40 return, $28 one-way), a 1.4km-long funicular railway, in operation since 1888. The eight-minute ascent tackles 27-degree slopes, forcing you back into your wooden bench as the carriages are steadily hauled through the forest. The ride begins at the terminal on Garden Road and finishes at the **Peak Tower**, an ugly concrete structure generally referred to as the Flying Wok. Its sole virtue is the superb views from the Sky Terrace – which they charge a further $35 to access – encompassing the harbour, Tsim Sha Tsui's land reclamation projects and low-tech concrete tower blocks, right into the New Territories. **Free vistas** can be savoured from the lookout 100m past the tower, or across the road, from the upper terrace of the **Peak Galleria**, a touristy complex full of shops and restaurants. It's a panorama that's difficult to tire of – come up again at night when the lights of Hong Kong transform the city into a glittering box of tricks.

You're not yet at the top of The Peak itself: four roads pan out from the tower, one of which, **Mount Austin Road**, provides a stiff twenty-minute walk up to **Victoria Peak Garden**. Alternatively, a **circuit** of The Peak via shady **Harlech Road** takes around an hour. First views are of Aberdeen and Lamma; later, as you turn into Lugard Road, Kowloon and Central come into sight. You can also **walk back to Central** from The Peak Tower in around forty minutes, via the **Old Peak Road**, a surfaced but steep track which descends through the forest and past Central's uppermost apartments, to emerge onto Robinson Road near the zoo.

MAN MO TEMPLE

HOLLYWOOD ROAD

Ⓜ Central, Exit D2/Sheung Wan, Exit A2.
MAP P.32–33, POCKET MAP B5-C6

Hollywood Road, and the streets nearby, form a run of antique shops, curio sellers and furniture stores. There are some wonderful furnishings and artworks here – old and new ceramics, burial pottery, painted screens, prints, jewellery and embroidery – and a group of more upmarket antique shops at the eastern end. Further west, the selection becomes more mixed (and prices lower), with smaller places and pavement vendors selling bric-a-brac on parallel **Upper Lascar Row**. In Victorian times this market was infamous for its thieves and dubbed "Cat Street" by the white population (after "cat burglar", according to some).

MAN MO TEMPLE

Hollywood Rd Ⓜ Sheung Wan, Exit A2. Daily 8am–6pm. Free. MAP P.32–33, POCKET MAP B5

The Man Mo Temple is one of Hong Kong's oldest, built in the 1840s and equipped with decorations from mainland China, all hung with smouldering incense spirals. The temple's name derives from the words for "civil" (*man*) and "martial" (*mo*): the first attribute belongs to the god of literature, Man Cheong, who protects civil servants (he's the red-robed statue wielding a writing brush); the latter to the martial deity, Kuan Ti (represented by another statue, in green, holding a sword). Kuan Ti is based on the real-life warrior Kuan Yu of the Three Kingdoms Period (around 220 AD), who is protector of pawnshops, policemen, secret societies and the military.

SHEUNG WAN

Ⓜ Sheung Wan. MAP P.32–33, POCKET MAP C5

Sheung Wan begins pretty much west of Jubilee Street, and though modern development has torn out many of the **old lanes** and their street vendors, a few – such as Wing Kut Street and Man Wa Lane – survive, and are full of stalls hawking calligraphy brushes, clothes and carved name stamps, or "chops". Sheung Wan's most distinctive structure is the **Shun Tak Centre**; set on

The Mid-Levels Escalator

The **Mid-Levels Escalator** cuts up the hillside for 800m from the footbridge across Queen's Road by the corner of Jubilee Street, via Hollywood Road and the popular restaurant district of **Soho**, ending at Conduit Road. It carries thirty thousand commuters daily on a one-way system, which runs uphill from 10.20am to midnight, and downhill from 6am to 10am (use accompanying staircases to go against the flow). All told, it's a twenty-minute ride from bottom to top, or 45 minutes if you have to walk.

Medicinal tea

Medicinal tea is an integral part of Chinese life, and is sold from open-fronted shops where cups or bowls are ranged on a counter alongside ornate brass urns, each hung with a label naming the concoction in Chinese. Despite the name, these brews are made not from tea leaves but from various astringent medicinal herbs, and – like most medicines – need to be drunk down in one gulp before you've had a chance to taste them. Popular in winter for driving off colds are *ng fa cha* (five-flower tea) and *ya sei mei* (twenty-four flavour tea).

the waterfront on Connaught Road, its twin towers are encased in a distinctive red framework and house the Macau Ferry Terminal. Opposite is the **Western Market** (daily 10am–7pm), whose fine Edwardian brick-and ironwork shell houses two floors of fabric shops. For a modern, multi-storey Chinese produce market – involving vast amounts of fruit, vegetables and freshly slaughtered meat – try **Sheung Wan Market** on Morrison Street; the second floor is a mass of stalls (daily 6am–2am) serving all sorts of light meals.

The streets due west of here provide glimpses of the trades and industries that date back to Hong Kong's settlement. Many shops on Wing Lok Street and Bonham Strand specialize in **bird's nest** and **ginseng**. The nests are used to make bird's nest soup, a gastronomic speciality said to promote longevity; as the nest is tasteless, however, the dish's quality rests in the soup itself. Ginseng, the root of a plant found in Southeast Asia and North America, is prescribed for a whole host of problems, from reviving mental faculties in the aged, to curing impotence – some of the larger ginseng trading companies have venerable interiors decked out in teak and glass panels. Many shops in Ko Shing Street are dedicated wholesalers, selling **traditional Chinese medicines** such as deer antlers, crushed pearls, dried seahorses and assorted herbalists' paraphernalia. Others lean towards kitchen supplies with their piles of dried mushrooms, salted and preserved fish, dried squid, oysters, sea slugs, scallops and seaweed.

Shops

BLANC DE CHINE

Shop 123, Landmark Building, Central
Ⓜ Central, Exit K. MAP P.32–33, POCKET MAP E6

Elegant and expensive
designs for men and women
loosely based on traditional
Chinese clothes, mostly in silk
or cashmere.

BOOKAZINE

Prince's Building, 10 Chater Rd Ⓜ Central,
Exit K. Mon–Sat 9.30am–7.30pm. MAP P.32–33,
POCKET MAP E5

Bookshop with a large
collection on Hong Kong and
China, from glossy coffee-table
works to novels, local maps and
hiking guides.

DRAGON CULTURE

231 Hollywood Rd, Sheung Wan Ⓜ Sheung
Wan, Exit A2. Mon–Sat 10am–6pm.
MAP P.32–33, POCKET MAP B5

Upmarket Chinese antiques,
including pottery, porcelain and
bronzeware; a good place to
find museum-quality artefacts.

SHOPPING IN CENTRAL

EU YAN SANG

152–156 Queen's Rd, Central Ⓜ Sheung
Wan, Exit E2. Mon–Sat 10am–2pm and
3–7pm. MAP P.32–33, POCKET MAP C5

Hong Kong's most famous
medicine shop, founded in
1879, and now with branches
right across Southeast Asia.
A source of teas, herbs and
Chinese medicines, all carefully
weighed and measured.

FLOW

29 Lyndhurst Terrace, Central Ⓜ Central,
Exit D2. Daily noon–7.30pm. MAP P.32–33,
POCKET MAP C6

The city's best secondhand
bookshop, full of everything
from holiday pulp to
coffee-table albums and DVDs.
Takes time to sort through the
crowded shelves.

HONEYCHURCH ANTIQUES

29 Hollywood Rd, Central Ⓜ Central, Exit
D2. Call ☎ 2541 3683 for opening times.
MAP P.32–33, POCKET MAP C6

Long-established gallery
offering a selection of unusual,
expensive curios, including
silver, books and prints.

KARIN WEBER GALLERY

20 Aberdeen St, Central Ⓜ Sheung Wan,
Exit A2. Tues–Sat 11am–7pm. MAP P.32–33,
POCKET MAP C5

Large selection of mid-price
contemporary fine art and
regular pieces of antique
furniture; they also organize
furniture-buying trips to
warehouses on the mainland.

LANE CRAWFORD

IFC Mall, Central Ⓜ Central, Exit F. Daily
10am–9pm. MAP P.32–33, POCKET MAP E5

Hong Kong's oldest Western-
style department store,
locally dubbed "Hong Kong
Harrods" and similarly
upmarket. Worth checking
for seasonal sales.

LINVA TAILOR

38 Cochrane St, Central Ⓜ Central, Exit D2.
MAP P.32-33, POCKET MAP C6
Well-established ladies' tailor,
popular with locals who want
cheongsams for parties. They
work a lot with embroidery.

MARGARET COURT TAILORESS

8/F, Winner Building, 27 D'Aguilar St, Lan
Kwai Fong Ⓜ Central, Exit D2. MAP P.37.
SEE INSET ON POCKET MAP B7
Margaret Court has lots of local
Western female clients, and a
solid reputation for good work,
although it certainly doesn't
come cheap.

SHANGHAI TANG

1 Duddell St, Central Ⓜ Central, Exit D2.
Daily 10.30am–8pm. MAP P.32-33, POCKET MAP D6
Beautifully done up in 1930s
Shanghai style, this store
specializes in new versions of
traditional Chinese clothing –
often in their trademark
combination of pink, green and
black silk – and they also offer
a made-to-order service. It's
expensive, but the good, and
regular, sales are definitely
worth a look.

TERESA COLEMAN

55 Wyndham St, Soho Ⓜ Central, Exit D2.
Call for appointment. ☎ 2530 4863. MAP P.37.
SEE INSET ON POCKET MAP A7
Specialist in antique textiles,
including Tibetan rugs and
thangkas, Chinese silk robes
and ethnic embroideries.

TRUE ARTS AND CURIOS

91 Hollywood Rd, Sheung Wan Ⓜ Central,
Exit D2. MAP P.32-33, POCKET MAP C5
Tiny place crammed to the
rafters with a mix of tourist
trinkets and genuine antiques.
Good for a souvenir.

WATTIS FINE ART

20 Hollywood Rd, Central Ⓜ Central, Exit D2.
Mon–Sat 10am–6pm. MAP P.32-33, POCKET MAP C6

LOK CHA TEA HOUSE

An intriguing cave, full of
China-related old maps,
paintings and prints. Don't
expect bargains – these are
collector's prices – but it's a
fascinating place for a browse.

WING ON

211 Des Voeux Rd Ⓜ Sheung Wan, Exit A1.
Daily 9am–6pm. MAP P.32-33, POCKET MAP C5
Long-established Chinese
department store selling
standard day-to-day goods.

YUE PO CHAI ANTIQUES

132–134 Hollywood Rd, Central Ⓜ Sheung
Wan, Exit A2. MAP P.32-33, POCKET MAP B5
Browse through this maze of
dusty pots, jars, plates and
ephemera, and, among
good-looking reproductions,
you'll find some genuine
antiques.

Restaurants

BEP

9–11 Staunton St, Central Ⓜ Central, Exit
D2 ☎ 2522 7533. Daily noon–4pm & 6–11pm.
MAP P.32-33, POCKET MAP C6
Excellent Vietnamese food,
cramped seating and unusually
good service for Hong Kong.
The tomato and crab soup, *pho*
and *rau cuon* rolls are the
dishes of choice. $100 a head.

MAN WAH

seafood – rock oysters, fish and chips, scallops and char-grilled sardines. They do good breakfasts too.

CAFÉ DECO

Peak Galleria, 118 Peak Rd, The Peak
☎ 2849 5111. Sun–Thurs 11am–11pm, Fri & Sat 11am–11.30pm. MAP P.32–33, POCKET MAP B9

Exceptional views and a stylish Art Deco interior. The menu includes seafood, sushi, tapas and grills, or you can just have cake and coffee – there's often also live jazz. The location ensures relatively high prices. Book for window seats.

DAN DAN SOUL FOOD

Grand Millennium Plaza, 181 Queen's Road Central, Sheung Wan ⓜSheung Wan, Exit E2. Daily 11.30am–9pm. MAP P.32–33, POCKET MAP C5

Home-style Sichuanese food with bite: try the signature spicy *dandan* noodles, *zhong* dumplings, cucumber with vinegar-garlic sauce or dumplings of the day. Around $150 a head.

DOT COD

Basement, Prince's Building, 10 Chater Rd, Central ⓜ Central, Exit K ☎ 2810 6988. Mon–Sat 7.30am–11.30pm. MAP P.32–33, POCKET MAP E6

A chic, pricey place to eat fairly straightforward British-style

FLYING PAN

9 Old Bailey St, Soho ⓜ Central, Exit D2 ☎ 2140 6333. Daily 24hr. MAP P.32–33, POCKET MAP C6

All-day breakfast fry-ups, with generous portions of almost unlimited combinations of eggs, bacon, burgers, beans, sausages, tomatoes and mushrooms. Their coffee isn't the best, but it's a great place to start the day.

FUNG SHING

G/F, 7 On Tai St, Sheung Wan ⓜ Sheung Wan, Exit A1 ☎ 2815 8689. Daily 7am–11pm. MAP P.32–33, POCKET MAP B4

Signed in Chinese below the more obvious Treasure Lake restaurant, this friendly place serves excellent, inexpensive Shunde-style *dim sum* – try honey-roast pork or paper-thin *sheung fan*.

ISLAND TANG

Shop 222, The Galleria, 9 Queen's Road Central, ⓜ Central, Exit K ☎ 2526 8798. MAP P.32–33 POCKET MAP D6

Suave interior sporting a 1920s Chinese-colonial look – dark wooden panels, starched white tablecloths and a plush carpet. The menu offers chic, small portions of bird's nest soup, Chinese seafood and *dim sum*. Expensive.

IVAN THE KOZAK

G/F, 46–48 Cochrane St ⓜ Central, Exit D2 ☎ 2851 1193. Mon–Fri noon–midnight, Sat & Sun 6pm–midnight. MAP P.32–33, POCKET MAP C6

Chicken Kiev, lamb stew and lots of cabbage and potatoes. Portions are decent, good value and tasty, but the highlight here is donning a fur coat and walking into the huge freezer for a shot of vodka and a photo.

LA PAMPA

32 Staunton St, Soho Ⓜ Central, Exit D2
☎ 2868 6959. Mon–Fri noon–2.30pm &
6–11pm, Sat & Sun noon–5pm & 6–11pm.
MAP P.32–33, POCKET MAP C6

Blow out on moderately
expensive Argentinean steak,
in upwards of 250g portions,
grilled to your instructions and
served with nominal quantities
of vegetables.

LIN HEUNG TEA HOUSE

160–164 Wellington St, Sheung Wan
Ⓜ Sheung Wan, Exit A2 ☎ 2544 4556. Daily
6am–11pm, *dim sum* served until 4pm.
MAP P.32–33, POCKET MAP C5

This popular, inexpensive *dim
sum* restaurant relocated here
from Guangzhou (in China)
around 1950, and they've been
so busy since, they haven't had
time to change the furnishings
or allow their ancient staff to
retire. Brusque atmosphere with
plain, good food. Crowds queue
up for their Mid-Autumn
Festival mooncakes.

MAN WAH

LOK CHA TEA HOUSE

K.C. Lo Gallery, Hong Kong Park, Central
Ⓜ Admiralty, Exit C1 ☎ 2801 7177. Daily
10am–8pm, closed second Tues of the month.
MAP P.32–33, POCKET MAP F7

Elegant place furnished with
carved Chinese screens and
wooden tables, serving
vegetarian *dim sum* and
specialist Chinese teas – all
brewed and served differently.
Aimed at tourists rather than
locals, though excellent quality;
expect to pay $100 a head.

LUK YU TEA HOUSE

24–26 Stanley St, just west of D'Aguilar St,
Central Ⓜ Central, Exit D2 ☎ 2523 5464.
Daily 7am–10pm. MAP P.32–33, POCKET MAP D6

A snapshot from the 1930s,
with old wooden furniture and
ceiling fans, this self-consciously
traditional restaurant's mainstay
is *dim sum*. Despite local fame,
the food, though good quality,
barely justifies its tourist-inflated
prices. Upwards of $100 a head.

MAN WAH

25/F, Mandarin Oriental Hotel, 5 Connaught
Rd Ⓜ Central, Exit F ☎ 2825 4003. Daily
noon–3pm & 6.30–11pm. MAP P.32–33,
POCKET MAP E6

Subtle and accomplished *dim
sum* and southern Chinese
food at connoisseurs' prices
($700 a head and up), though
the stunning harbour views
outperform the menu.

THE PEAK LOOKOUT

121 Peak Rd, The Peak ☎ 2849
1000. Mon–Thurs 10.30am–11.30pm, Fri & Sat
10.30am–1am, Sun 8.30am–11pm. MAP P.32–33,
POCKET MAP B9

The stone colonial building
with raked ceilings makes a
nice setting for working your
way through their Asian-Indian
menu. Pricey, but reasonable
value for brunch or alfresco
night-time dining. Reckon on
around $350 per head.

SAM TOR

30 Pottinger St, Central Ⓜ Central, Exit D2
☎ 2801 6352. Daily 11am–7pm. MAP P.32–33,
POCKET MAP D6

Originally famous for its "white cooked" goose innards (very crunchy; HK$60), many now opt for their wonton noodle soup (HK$28 a bowl). Get in before noon if you don't want to join the huge queue.

TAI CHEONG BAKERY

35 Lyndhurst Terrace, Central Ⓜ Central,
Exit D2 ☎ 2544 3475. Daily 7.30am–9pm. MAP
P.32–33, POCKET MAP C6

You wouldn't know it from the Chinese-only sign and basic tiled interior, but this tiny estab-lishment was founded in 1954 and has since spawned a Hong Kong-wide chain. Best for Hong Kong-style egg tarts (not grilled like Macau's version; $6) and flaky char siu pastries ($9).

TSIM CHAI KEE NOODLE

98 Wellington St, Central Ⓜ Central, Exit D2
☎ 2850 6471. Daily 11am–9.30pm. MAP P.32–33,
POCKET MAP D6

This place is easily located by the lunchtime queue tailing downhill. It's definitely worth the wait, and even worth being jammed into the packed interior, for the famous wonton – jokingly known locally as "ping-pong wonton" because of their huge size – served in soup for just $28.

TSUI WAH

17–19 Wellington St, Central Ⓜ Central,
Exit D2 ☎ 2525 6338. Daily 24hr. MAP P.37,
SEE INSET ON POCKET MAP B6

Multistorey institution serving a huge array of inexpensive Cantonese fast food, but the fishball noodle soup is the thing to go for, along with Hai Nam chicken or the very sweet desserts. Extremely busy at lunchtimes.

YUNG KEE

32–40 Wellington St, Central Ⓜ Central,
Exit D2 ☎ 2522 1624. Daily 11am–11pm. MAP
P.37, SEE INSET ON POCKET MAP B6

A Hong Kong institution with a Michelin star, serving classic Cantonese food. Their roast pork and goose are superb, or try the set meals from $360.

Bars and clubs

BIT POINT

46–48 Wyndham St, Lan Kwai Fong
Ⓜ Central, Exit D2 ☎ 2523 7436. Mon–Fri
noon–2am, Sat & Sun 5pm–2am; happy hour
4–9pm. MAP P.37, SEE INSET ON POCKET MAP A7

German theme bar serving meals until around 10pm, after which the bar starts selling industrial quantities of lager and schnapps.

BOUJIS

37 Pottinger St, Central Ⓜ Central,
Exit D2 ☎ 2323 0200. Wed–Sat 10pm–late.
MAP P.32–33, POCKET MAP C5

Sleek nightclub chain, featuring a line-up of international DJs, a cocktail lounge, dancefloor and – of course – an exclusive VIP area with viewing deck.

CLUB 71

67 Hollywood Rd, Central Ⓜ Sheung Wan,
Exit A2 ☎ 2858 7071. Daily 5pm–late.
MAP P.32–33, POCKET MAP C5

This tiny, hard-to-find bohemian place has a reasonably priced happy hour and a front-of-house terrace. Look for 69 Hollywood Road and take the small lane around the back.

D26

26 D'Aguilar St, Lan Kwai Fong Ⓜ Central, Exit
D2 ☎ 2877 1610. Mon–Fri 2pm–1.30am, Sat
5pm–3am. MAP P.37, SEE INSET ON POCKET MAP B7

Small, low-key bar – a good place for a warm-up drink or if you actually want to have a conversation. Good-value set lunches in the week.

FRINGE CLUB

2 Lower Albert Rd Ⓜ Central, Exit D2
☎ 2521 7251. Mon–Thurs noon–midnight, Fri & Sat noon–3am; happy hour 4–9pm. MAP P.37, SEE INSET ON POCKET MAP B7

The ground-floor bar of this theatre and art-gallery complex has good-value beers and live music, and there's also a popular rooftop bar.

HAVANA BAR

4/F, The Plaza, 21 D'Aguilar Street, Lan Kwai Fong Ⓜ Central, Exit D2 ☎ 2851 4880. Mon–Sat 6pm–2am. MAP P.37, SEE INSET ON POCKET MAP B7

This popular bar offers a reprieve from Lan Kwai Fong's evening crowds, with a spacious terrace and the largest selection of rum in the city. Good tapas too.

INSOMNIA

38–44 D'Aguilar St, Lan Kwai Fong Ⓜ Central, Exit D2 ☎ 2525 0957. 24hr; happy hour 8am–9pm. MAP P.37, SEE INSET ON POCKET MAP A7

Street-side bar where, early in the evening, conversation is possible. Later, the house band plays covers at full volume.

KEG SPORTS BAR

52 D'Aguilar St Ⓜ Central, Exit D2 ☎ 2810 0369. Sun–Thurs 5pm–1am, Fri & Sat 5pm–2am. MAP P.37, SEE INSET ON POCKET MAP A7

Decked out in wood and metal trim to resemble the inside of a barrel, this place has a range of imported beers, including Ruddles and Hoegaarden. Popular with British expats.

LE JARDIN

10 Wing Wah Lane, Lan Kwai Fong Ⓜ Central, Exit D2 ☎ 2526 2717. Mon–Fri 4.30pm–late, Sat 5pm–late. MAP P.37, SEE INSET ON POCKET MAP A6

Tiny terrace bar hidden away up a flight of steps at the end of Wing Wah Lane. A relaxed spot for those in the know to kick off an evening with a few drinks.

MAGNUM CLUB

1 Wellington St Ⓜ Central, Exit D2 ☎ 2116 1602. Mon–Sat 10pm–2am. MAP P.37, SEE INSET ON POCKET MAP B7

Huge bar and DJ-driven dance venue on three floors (plus gold-plated bathrooms and an outdoor terrace), one of which is for VIPs only.

NOVA

2 & 3/F, Lyndhurst Tower, 1 Lyndhurst Terrace Ⓜ Central, Exit D2 ☎ 2522 2608. Sun–Thurs 9.30am–1am, Fri & Sat 9.30am–2.30am. MAP P.32–33, POCKET MAP D6

Club and bar whose interior, all angles and floor-level lighting, looks lifted from *2001: A Space Odyssey*. There's a lounge bar and outdoor terraces upsairs, and DJs play in the club at the weekends.

ORIGIN

G/F, 48 Wyndham St Ⓜ Central, Exit D2 ☎ 2668 5583. Mon–Sat 5pm–3am. MAP P.37, SEE INSET ON POCKET MAP A7

Brick and exposed dark timber interior lend tropical ambiance to what is, essentially, a very stylish gin bar, serving Mother's Ruin in a bewildering variety of cocktails.

LE JARDIN

Hong Kong Island: Wan Chai, Causeway Bay and Happy Valley

Wan Chai and Causeway Bay stretch 4km east from Central along Hong Kong Island's north shore. With high-rises and congested expressways in all directions, this isn't a pretty area, though packed with eating, drinking and shopping opportunities. Wan Chai's enduring reputation for seedy bars was immortalized in Richard Mason's 1957 novel, *The World of Suzie Wong*, but the area has some architectural gems and even a semi-rural walk to offer. Further east, Causeway Bay is a lively spread of shops, parks and restaurants, though land reclamation has made a joke of the name – the only surviving maritime feature is a typhoon shelter. To the south, Happy Valley is worth a trip on Wednesday evenings to take in the atmosphere of the horse races – Hong Kong's only legal betting outlet.

THE CONVENTION AND EXHIBITION CENTRE

Convention Avenue Ⓜ Wan Chai, Exit A1. MAP P.50–51, POCKET MAP H5

Of all the huge buildings looming over Wan Chai's harbourfront, the weirdest is the Convention and Exhibition Centre, whose curve-roofed **CEC Extension** resembles a giant manta ray. This was where the British formally handed Hong Kong back to China in June 1997, and as such is a huge draw with Chinese tourists who come to pose beside the golden **Forever Blooming Bauhinia Sculpture** on the harbourside terrace. The orchid-like bauhinia flower was adopted as the SAR's regional emblem in 1997, its five petals appearing on Hong Kong's red flag. You can catch a cross-harbour ferry (daily 7.30am–10.50pm; every 10min; $2.50) to Tsim Sha Tsui from the **Wan Chai Star Ferry Pier**, just east of the Exhibition Centre.

CENTRAL PLAZA

Harbour Rd Ⓜ Wan Chai, Exit A1. MAP P.50–51, POCKET MAP H6

Sited opposite the Convention and Exhibition Centre, Central Plaza is another notable architectural marvel – it's the world's tallest building made of reinforced concrete (374m). Triangular in shape, it's topped by a glass pyramid from which a 64m mast protrudes: the locals dubbed it "The Big Syringe". It's lit at night by luminous neon panels, while the spire on top of the pyramid has four sections that change colour every fifteen minutes to show the time.

There's a **public viewing bay** on the 46th floor (Mon–Fri 8am–8pm; free), which comprises a whole floor of giant windows where you can get a walk-around 360-degree view over the harbour and neighbouring buildings.

QUEEN'S ROAD EAST

Ⓜ Admiralty, Exit J. MAP P.50-51, POCKET MAP G7–K8

Inland, up against The Peak's foothills, **Queen's Road East** features a concentration of furniture stores, many offering fine-quality reproduction antique Chinese wooden chairs, screens and tables. Around halfway down the road, steps on **Ship Street** climb to supposedly haunted **Nam Koo Terrace**, though – aside from an abundance of stray cats and an old stone mansion – there's little to see. The nearby **Hung Shing Temple** occupies a natural grotto right on the roadside and is dedicated to a mix of Chinese gods, including Hung Shing himself, a deified Tang dynasty official who was able to forecast the weather.

A short way further east is the cylindrical **Hopewell Centre**, which features a revolving restaurant on its upper levels, and the **Old Wan Chai Post Office**, built in 1915 and now the headquarters for an environmental agency. Across the road, **Tai Yuen Street** hosts a crowded outdoor market selling all manner of household goods, food and cheap clothing.

Back on Queen's Road East, **Stone Nullah Lane**, a nondescript little street, heads uphill to the splendid **Pak Tai Temple** (daily 8am–5pm). Surrounded by tall trees and with woodland above, the temple is crowned in decorative

LOVERS ROCK

roof tiles, featuring operatically posed figures from Chinese folklore and mythology. Pak Tai, the Northern Emperor, is considered a guardian against flooding, and a seventeenth-century copper statue inside the temple shows him overpowering evil forces in the shape of a turtle and snake.

BOWEN ROAD AND LOVERS ROCK

Ⓜ Wan Chai. POCKET MAP H9/J9

It's a stiff hike up lanes from beside the Old Wan Chai Post Office or Pak Tai Temple to **Bowen Road**, a level pedestrian path among the thick forest above Wan Chai, offering occasional glimpses of the city through the canopy. It's a popular spot with walkers and joggers, and is amazingly wild given its location just minutes from Wan Chai's busy expressways – watch out for snakes along the path. Walk east and you'll soon come to steps ascending to **Lovers Rock**, a huge stone boulder pointing rudely skywards above the trees, draped in festive red ribbons and a popular pilgrimage spot for young women during the annual Maidens' Festival.

THE NOON DAY GUN

THE NOON DAY GUN

Gloucester Rd Ⓜ Causeway Bay, Exit D1.
MAP P.50–51, POCKET MAP L6

Causeway Bay's sole visible colonial relic is a small ship's cannon known as the Noon Day Gun, celebrated in Noel Coward's song *Mad Dogs and Englishmen*, and which is, even today, detonated daily at noon by a smartly dressed officer. There are many stories to explain why, none of them remotely convincing. Unless you catch the actual event, the gun itself is underwhelming; get here via the subway from the car park next to the *Excelsior Hotel* opposite.

VICTORIA PARK

Ⓜ Causeway Bay, Exit E. 24hr. MAP P.50–51,
POCKET MAP M6

Sited east of Gloucester Road, Victoria Park is a flat, spacious spread of paving, sports fields and ornamental borders. It's busy around the clock, with martial arts practitioners and old men airing their caged songbirds at the crack of dawn, people cooling off on benches under the trees at midday, and football matches in the afternoon. A couple of times a year the park hosts some lively festivals, including a flower market at Chinese New Year, a lantern display for the

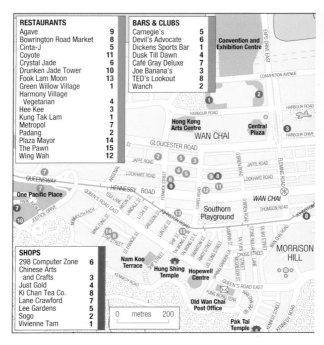

RESTAURANTS	
Agave	9
Bowrington Road Market	
Cinta-J	5
Coyote	11
Crystal Jade	6
Drunken Jade Tower	10
Fook Lam Moon	13
Green Willow Village	1
Harmony Village Vegetarian	4
Hee Kee	3
Kung Tak Lam	1
Metropol	7
Padang	2
Plaza Mayor	14
The Pawn	15
Wing Wah	12

BARS & CLUBS	
Carnegie's	5
Devil's Advocate	6
Dickens Sports Bar	1
Dusk Till Dawn	4
Café Gray Deluxe	7
Joe Banana's	3
TED's Lookout	8
Wanch	2

SHOPS	
298 Computer Zone	6
Chinese Arts and Crafts	3
Just Gold	4
Ki Chan Tea Co.	8
Lane Crawford	7
Lee Gardens	5
Sogo	2
Vivienne Tam	1

Mid-Autumn Festival and the annual candlelit vigil for the victims of Tiananmen Square on June 4.

TIMES SQUARE

Ⓜ Causeway Bay, Exit A. MAP P.50–51, POCKET MAP K7

The most startling fixture in the Causeway Bay shopping area is the beige blockbuster of a building that is Times Square, at the corner of Matheson and Russell streets. Spearing skywards, it exemplifies Hong Kong's modern architecture, where only vertical space is available and distinction is attained by unexpected design – in this case, a monolithic shopping mall supported by great marble trunks and featuring a cathedral window and giant video advertising screen. At ground level there's a cinema and direct access to the MTR; there are also plenty of pricey restaurants inside.

TIMES SQUARE

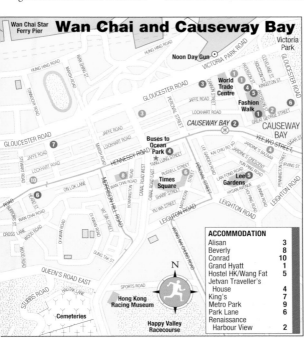

Wan Chai and Causeway Bay

Wan Chai Star Ferry Pier

Victoria Park

Noon Day Gun

GLOUCESTER ROAD

World Trade Centre

Fashion Walk

CAUSEWAY BAY Ⓜ

CAUSEWAY BAY

GLOUCESTER ROAD

JAFFE ROAD

Buses to Ocean Park

Times Square

Lee Gardens

LEIGHTON ROAD

LEIGHTON ROAD

QUEEN'S ROAD EAST

Hong Kong Racing Museum

Cemeteries

Happy Valley Racecourse

N

ACCOMMODATION	
Alisan	3
Beverly	8
Conrad	10
Grand Hyatt	1
Hostel HK/Wang Fat	5
Jetvan Traveller's House	4
King's	7
Metro Park	9
Park Lane	6
Renaissance Harbour View	2

HAPPY VALLEY RACECOURSE

Ⓜ Causeway Bay Ⓦ happyvalleyracecourse.com. MAP P.50–51, POCKET MAP K8–L9

Once a malarial swamp, initially settled, then abandoned, by the British, Happy Valley – or *pau ma dei*, "horseracing track" in Cantonese – means one thing only to locals: gambling. All other forms of betting are banned in Hong Kong, and the Happy Valley Racecourse is the traditional centre of this multi-million-dollar business, with a second track at Sha Tin in the New Territories. It's controlled by the Hong Kong Jockey Club, one of the colony's power bastions since its foundation in 1884, with a board of stewards made up of the leading lights of Hong Kong big business. A percentage of the profits go to social and charitable causes – including funding for many hospitals – and such is the passion for betting in Hong Kong that the racing season pulls in over $80 billion per year.

The season runs from September to mid-June and there are usually meetings every Wednesday night, an intense experience with the crowds packed into the high stands surrounding the tight track. Entrance to the public enclosure is $10; there you can mix with a beery expat crowd, watch the horses being paraded before each race, and pump the staff to make sense of the intricate accumulator bets that Hong Kong bookies specialize in. Other options include joining the hard-bitten Chinese punters up in the stands, mostly watching the action on television ($20, plus all the cigarette smoke and Cantonese cursing you can handle), or signing up for the Hong Kong Tourist Board's **Come Horseracing Tour** (from $1200 depending on the event), which will take you to the course, feed you before the races, get you into the members' enclosure and provide some racing tips. You need to be over 18 and have been in Hong Kong for less than three weeks – take your passport to any HK tourist office at least a day before the race.

On the second floor of the main building at the racecourse, the **Hong Kong**

Racing Museum (daily noon–7pm; free) presents various aspects of Hong Kong's racing history, from the early days in Happy Valley through to the various charitable projects funded by the Jockey Club. Racing buffs can also study champion racehorse characteristics and famous jockeys in the museum's eight galleries and cinema.

THE CEMETERIES

Wong Nai Chung Rd Ⓜ Causeway Bay. Daily 8am–5pm. Free. MAP P.50–51, POCKET MAP J8–K9

The series of terraced hillside cemeteries west of the racecourse provides an interesting snapshot of the territory's ethnic and religious mix during its earliest days, with separate enclosures for Muslim, Catholic, Protestant, Parsee and Jewish inhabitants. The large Protestant cemetery is probably the most interesting, full of shady fig trees and grandiose granite monuments dating back to the 1850s, and a bit wild and overgrown towards the corners. It's noteworthy that just about everyone buried here before the 1950s seems to have died prematurely, often in virulent epidemics – probably because fewer expatriates lived permanently in Hong Kong before this time, and would have returned home after retiring.

MUSEUM OF COASTAL DEFENCE

Ⓜ Shau Kei Wan/tram or bus #2 from Central to Shau Kei Wan, then a signed 1km walk along Shau Kei Wan Main St Ⓦ hk. coastaldefence.museum. Daily except Thurs 10am–5pm. $10, free on Wed. POCKET MAP M5

Actually some way east from Causeway Bay, the Museum of Coastal Defence occupies the site of the Lei Yue Mun Fort,

EXHIBITS AT THE MUSEUM OF COASTAL DEFENCE

built by the British in 1887 to defend Victoria Harbour. Set high up on a hillside overlooking **Lei Yue Mun** – the "Carp Gate", Victoria Harbour's narrowest point – the bulk of the museum is in the renovated redoubt, the exhibition rooms reached by a maze of brick tunnels. The museum covers all stages of Hong Kong's maritime history, and exhibits include an opium-pipe display, moving letters from prisoners of war under the Japanese, and the richly embroidered satin army uniforms of Ming and Qing dynasty soldiers, studded with iron rivets. It's all fascinating, but also – unless you have a special interest in military history – probably a bit overwhelming. Outside, accompanied by stunning views of the rugged eastern end of Victoria Harbour, there's a marked trail past restored gun emplacements, underground magazines, a torpedo station and a gunpowder factory.

Shops

298 COMPUTER ZONE

298 Hennessy Rd, Wan Chai Ⓜ Wan Chai, Exit A4. MAP P.50–51, POCKET MAP J7

Despite the massive sign outside, it's hard to find the entrance to this warren-like place, full of booths selling new, secondhand, official and pirated computer gear on three levels. Reasonably priced accessories and software, though hardware is expensive.

CHINESE ARTS AND CRAFTS

26 Harbour Rd, Wan Chai Ⓜ Wan Chai, Exit A1. MAP P.50–51, POCKET MAP J6

A good selection of all types and qualities of china in traditional styles, plus a few antique pieces – some items are very good value.

JUST GOLD

452 Hennessy Rd, Wan Chai Ⓜ Causeway Bay, Exit B. MAP P.50–51, POCKET MAP K6

Local chain specializing in fun, fashionable, cheapish jewellery designs for young women.

SHOPPING AT TIMES SQUARE

KI CHAN TEA CO.

174 Johnston Rd, Wan Chai Ⓜ Wan Chai, Exit A3. MAP P.50–51, POCKET MAP J7

Old men distribute the tea leaves from their red-and-gold cylinders in this no-nonsense, well-established shop.

LANE CRAWFORD

Shop 126, Pacific Place 2, 88 Queensway, Wan Chai Ⓜ Admiralty, Exit C1. MAP P.50–51, POCKET MAP F7

Hong Kong's longest-established upmarket clothing store, with a well-stocked inventory of smart – if sometimes stuffy – designer brands from around the globe.

LEE GARDENS

Yun Ping Rd, Causeway Bay Ⓜ Causeway Bay, Exit F. MAP P.50–51, POCKET MAP L7

Two huge towers housing upmarket shopping malls and a selection of good restaurants.

SOGO

555 Hennessy Rd, Causeway Bay Ⓜ Causeway Bay, Exit D. Daily 10am–10pm. MAP P.50–51, POCKET MAP L6

Hong Kong's first Japanese department store, an enormous complex on thirteen floors which seems to sell just about everything.

TIMES SQUARE

Russell St, Causeway Bay Ⓜ Causeway Bay, Exit A. MAP P.50–51, POCKET MAP K7

Over two hundred shops on sixteen floors, featuring all of Hong Kong's major brands, plus plenty of international ones as well.

VIVIENNE TAM

Shop G17, Fashion Walk, Gloucester Rd, Causeway Bay Ⓜ Causeway Bay, Exit A. MAP P.50–51, POCKET MAP L6

Funky shirts and dresses in David Hockney-meets-Vivienne Westwood style, often featuring Chairman Mao and other icons of the East. Pricey.

Restaurants

AGAVE

93 Lockhart Rd, Wan Chai Ⓜ Wan Chai, Exit C ☏ 2866 3228. Mon–Fri noon–2am, Sat & Sun noon–4am. MAP P.50-51, POCKET MAP H7

Superb selection of tequilas and tasty, if not so authentic, Mexican food of the tortilla, enchilada and taco variety.

BOWRINGTON ROAD MARKET

Bowrington Rd, Wan Chai Ⓜ Causeway Bay, Exit A. Daily 24hr. MAP P.50-51, POCKET MAP K7

A full-on, bustling Chinese produce market wedged in between busy roads and flyovers, with a cooked food area upstairs selling inexpensive one-dish meals and noodle soups.

CINTA-J

G/F, Malaysia Building, 69 Jaffe Rd, Wan Chai Ⓜ Wan Chai, Exit A1 ☏ 2529 6622. Mon–Fri 11am–3am, Sat & Sun 11am–5am. MAP P.50-51, POCKET MAP H7

Legendary Indonesian and Filipino restaurant-bar, with a fantastic live band after dark most nights. Their sweet chilli squid and sour fish soup are the genuine article.

COYOTE

114–120 Lockhart Rd, Wan Chai Ⓜ Wan Chai, Exit C ☏ 2861 2221. Daily noon–2am. MAP P.50-51, POCKET MAP H7

Lively Tex-Mex bar and grill with good barbecued ribs, full of margarita-quaffing patrons digging into plates of nachos and spicy pizzas.

CRYSTAL JADE

Basement 2, Times Square, Causeway Bay Ⓜ Causeway Bay, Exit A ☏ 2506 0080. Daily 11am–11pm. MAP P.50-51, POCKET MAP L7

Popular branch of a city-wide Shanghainese fast food chain, serving excellent *xiaolongbao* dumplings – steamed pork mince balls in a thin,

FOOK LAM MOON

wheat-dough wrapper, which tend to be full of scalding juice.

DRUNKEN JADE TOWER

289 Hennessy Rd, Causeway Bay Ⓜ Wan Chai, Exit A2 ☏ 2511 1848. Daily 7am–11pm. MAP P.50-51, POCKET MAP J7

Don't be put off by the lack of English signage (look for 醉瓊 樓酒家); this small restaurant serves great Hakka-style *dim sum* and one-pot set meals for around $150 a head.

FOOK LAM MOON

35–45 Johnston Rd, Wan Chai Ⓜ Wan Chai, Exit B ☏ 2866 0663. Daily 11.30am–3pm & 6–11pm. MAP P.50-51, POCKET MAP H7

Among Hong Kong's most famous Cantonese restaurants. House specialities include bird's nest in coconut milk, abalone, crispy piglet and crisp-skinned chicken. Count on $800 a head.

GREEN WILLOW VILLAGE

11/F, World Trade Centre, Causeway Bay Ⓜ Causeway Bay, Exit E ☏ 2881 6669. Daily 11.30am–3pm & 5.30pm–midnight. MAP P.50-51, POCKET MAP L6

Smart Shanghai restaurant featuring classic dishes such as soy-braised *dongpo* pork, lotus-leaf-wrapped pork, beggars' chicken (baked in mud) and braised stuffed duck.

HARMONY VILLAGE VEGETARIAN

11/F Jardine Centre, 50 Jardine's Bazaar, Causeway Bay Ⓜ Causeway Bay, Exit F ☎ 2881 5698. Daily 11.30am–11pm. MAP P.50–51, POCKET MAP L7

Buddhist vegetarian place – no onions or garlic – seating just fifteen, with a lunchtime set meal featuring unlimited rice for around $50.

HEE KEE

440 Jaffe Rd, Causeway Bay Ⓜ Causeway Bay, Exit C ☎ 2575 7565. Daily noon–midnight. MAP P.50–51, POCKET MAP K6

Minimalist location for consuming deep-fried whole crab with chillies, said to be an old Causeway Bay speciality. Sporadically popular with Hong Kong film stars.

KUNG TAK LAM

10/F, World Trade Centre, Causeway Bay Ⓜ Causeway Bay, Exit E ☎ 2890 3127. Daily 11am–11pm. MAP P.50–51, POCKET MAP L6

Shanghai-style vegetarian restaurant specializing in "meat" dishes, though the food – while tasty enough – is nowhere near as good as the view out over the harbour. Try to get a table by the window.

METROPOL

4/F, United Centre, 95 Queensway, Wan Chai Ⓜ Admiralty, Exit C1 ☎ 2865 1988. Daily 8am–midnight. MAP P.50–51, POCKET MAP F7

Huge place that still uses trollies to wheel the *dim sum* selection around – a dying sight in Hong Kong. Try the flaky *char siu* pastries and crunchy prawn dumplings.

PADANG

J.P. Plaza, 22–36 Paterson St, Causeway Bay Ⓜ Causeway Bay, Exit E ☎ 2881 5075. Daily 11am–11pm. MAP P.50–51, POCKET MAP L6

This unpretentious place does a good run of *rendang* (dry beef curry), satays, grilled seafood, mutton curry and – especially – durian-flavoured desserts. A little pricey for the portion sizes.

THE PAWN

62 Johnston Rd, Wan Chai Ⓜ Wan Chai, Exit A3 ☎ 2866 3444. Daily 11.30am–11pm. MAP P.50–51, POCKET MAP H7

Smart pub in an atmospherically-restored nineteenth-century Chinese pawnbroker's. Admire the views from the balcony or rooftop terrace, knock back a sundowner, and tuck into fish 'n' chips, ploughman's lunch and English breakfasts ($100–200).

PLAZA MAYOR

9 Moon St, Wan Chai Ⓜ Wan Chai, Exit B1 or B2 ☎ 2866 6644. Daily noon–midnight. MAP P.50–51, POCKET MAP G7

Tiny place with black-and-white tiling, a marble counter, excellent tapas – try the iberico ham and garlic shrimps – and good Spanish wine. $250 a head.

WING WAH

89 Hennessy Rd (there's no English sign), Wan Chai Ⓜ Wan Chai, Exit B ☎ 2527 7476. Mon–Sat noon–4am, Sun noon–1am. MAP P.50–51, POCKET MAP J7

Locally famous for its wonton noodle soup, which is what they'll bring you by default unless you ask for something else – such as their sweet red bean and tangerine peel soup.

Bars and clubs

CAFÉ GRAY DELUXE

Level 49, Pacific Place, 88 Queensway, Wan Chai Ⓜ Admiralty, Exit C1 ☎ 3968 1106. Daily 6.30am–10.30pm MAP P.50–51, POCKET MAP F7

The bar of this romantic restaurant is proof that the area has a greater choice of places to drink than its "sweaty dive" reputation suggests. Choose from their range of classic wines and cocktails, enjoy a bar snack and look out over the city.

CARNEGIE'S

53–55 Lockhart Rd, Wan Chai Ⓜ Wan Chai,
Exit C ☎ 2866 6289. Mon–Thurs 11am–late,
Sat noon–late, Sun 5pm–late. MAP P.50–51,
POCKET MAP H7

The noise level here means
conversation is only possible
by flash cards; once it's packed,
hordes of punters keen to
revel the night away fight for
dancing space on the bar. Hosts
the occasional riotous club
night and regular live music.

DEVIL'S ADVOCATE

48–50 Lockhart Rd, Wan Chai Ⓜ Wan Chai,
Exit C. Daily noon–1am. ☎ 2865 7271.
MAP P.50–51, POCKET MAP H7

Long-running, raucously
popular sports' bar which
attracts a younger crowd. If
you can cope with the terrible
1970s soundtrack, come along
during the happy hour (daily
noon–9pm) for excellent
deals or on Wednesdays for
further discounts.

DICKENS SPORTS BAR

Lower Ground Floor, *Excelsior Hotel*, 281
Gloucester Rd, Causeway Bay Ⓜ Causeway
Bay, Exit D1 ☎ 2837 6782. Mon–Thurs & Sun
11am–2am, Fri & Sat 11am–3am. MAP P.50–51,

POCKET MAP L6

This bar prides itself on
re-creating an authentic British
atmosphere: the kitchen dishes
up genuine British pub grub
(such as Yorkshire puddings
and mushy peas), the TV airs
British sitcoms, and there are
English papers to read.

DUSK TILL DAWN

76 Jaffe Rd, Wan Chai Ⓜ Wan Chai, Exit C
☎ 2528 4689. Mon–Sat noon–6am, Sun
3pm–6am; happy hour 5–11pm. MAP P.50–51,
POCKET MAP H7

Vaguely Mediterranean colours
decorate this rowdy bar, full of
loud live music, raucous staff
and hoarse punters.

JOE BANANAS

23 Luard Rd Ⓜ Wan Chai, Exit C ☎ 2529
1811. Mon–Fri noon–5am, Sat & Sun
5pm–5am. MAP P.50–51, POCKET MAP H7

Unsophisticated American bar
with a late disco, fake palms
and occasional live music. You
need to be (or look) 21 to get in
and there's a strict door policy
– men need a shirt with a collar.

TED'S LOOKOUT

G/F, Moonful Court, 17A Moon St, Wan Chai
Ⓜ Wan Chai, Exit B2 ☎ 5533 9369. Daily
noon–11pm. MAP P.50–51, POCKET MAP G7

Cute – or just plain small –
restaurant-bar in a quiet
cul-de-sac; the Tex-Mex style
food is above average, but the
drinks are superb, if pricey.

WANCH

54 Jaffe Rd Ⓜ Wan Chai, Exit C ☎ 2861
1621. Mon–Sat 11am–2am, Sun noon–2am.
MAP P.50–51, POCKET MAP G7

A Wan Chai institution, this
tiny, unpretentious bar is
jostling and friendly and has
live music – usually folk and
rock – every night. Also serves
cheap, chunky cheeseburgers
and sandwiches.

CARNEGIE'S

Hong Kong Island: the south side

Hong Kong Island's south side, while not undeveloped, still offers an escape from the north shore's densely packed high-rises. Aberdeen has a long maritime tradition, and the coastal stretch between here and the tourist enclave of Stanley is punctured by sandy bays and inlets, though you'll have to share them with crowds at the weekend. The beaches are pretty enough, however, and there's further distraction in one of Hong Kong's two theme parks – a great place to spend a day if you have kids in tow. The island's southeast corner has managed to remain as rural as anything can be on Hong Kong Island, featuring a bracing ridgetop hike, some almost wild coastal scenery and a superb beach out around Shek O.

ABERDEEN

Bus #7 from Outer Islands Ferry Pier, Central; #70 from Exchange Square, Central; or #72 from Moreton Terrace, Causeway Bay. MAP P.60-61

Aberdeen was already settled when the British arrived in the 1840s – the bay here was used by the indigenous Hoklos and Tankas, who fished in the surrounding archipelago. The harbour remains Aberdeen's focus, surrounded by a forest of tall apartment blocks and full of freshly cleaned fishing vessels during the July fishing moratorium – which is also when you can catch the annual **Dragon Boat Festival**.

Aberdeen's harbourside **fish market** (busiest before 10am) is an incredible sight, where trawlers disgorge their catches and have them sorted into rows of buckets, tanks and trays, among which wholesale buyers poke and prod. Some of the catch is recognisable, some downright unbelievable – bring a camera and, if you have them, waterproof shoes.

Along the waterfront you'll be approached by women selling **sampan rides** (about $50 per person after bargaining). These cruise the straits between Aberdeen and **Ap Lei Chau island** opposite – full of discount clothing warehouses – offering views of trawlers complete with dogs, drying laundry and outdoor kitchens. You can get a similar trip for free by catching the ferry from beside the fish market to one of Aberdeen's **floating restaurants**, moored around the side of Ap Lei Chau. The ostentatious *Jumbo* is the best-known (see p.63).

OCEAN PARK

Bus #629 from the Star Ferry Pier, Central ⓦ oceanpark.com.hk. Daily 10am–7pm. $345, under-11s $173; includes all rides and entry. MAP P.60-61

Filling a whole peninsula, Ocean Park is an open-air

ROLLERCOASTER AT OCEAN PARK

theme park and oceanarium; it also features four **giant pandas**, for whom a special two-thousand-square-metre complex has been created.

The first section, the Lowland area, is a landscaped garden with greenhouses, a butterfly house, a 3D-film simulator and a dinosaur discovery trail, with full-sized moving models. A **cable car** hoists you from here 1.5km up the mountain-side to the Headland section and its frightening Hair Raiser rollercoaster and the self-explanatory "Abyss Turbo Drop". There's also one of the world's largest reef aquariums, with a massive atoll that's home to more than two thousand fish, including giant rays and sharks. Looming over the lot is the **Ocean Park Tower**, 200m above sea level, giving superb vistas from its viewing platform and panoramic elevator. The **Tai Shue Wan** area below – linked by one of the longest outdoor escalators in the world – gives access to the Raging River Ride and the Middle Kingdom, a Chinese theme park with pagodas, traditional crafts and entertainment such as Chinese opera.

REPULSE BAY

Bus #6, #6A, #61, #64 or #260 from Exchange Square, Central. MAP P.60–61

Repulse Bay's name comes from the ship HMS *Repulse*, from which the British mopped up local pirates in the nineteenth century; during the colonial period the area was known for the cocktail parties held at the grand *Repulse Bay Hotel*. The hotel has since been demolished and **The Repulse Bay** erected on its remains, a wavy apartment block with a square hole through the centre, designed along *feng shui* principles (see p.35).

The beach is clean and wide, though on summer afternoons hordes of people descend on the sands. Connoisseurs of kitsch may want to amble down to the little Chinese garden at the end of the prom, where a brightly painted group of goddesses, Buddha statues, stone lions and dragons offer some tempting photo opportunities. If the crowds are too much, try the nearby beaches at **Middle Bay** and **South Bay**, fifteen minutes' and thirty minutes' walk south around the bay respectively.

STANLEY

Bus #6, #6A or #260 from Exchange Square, Central. MAP P.60–61

When Britain seized Hong Kong there were already two thousand people living at the south coast settlement of Stanley, earning an income from fishing and piracy. Today, it's a small residential place, with low-key modern buildings surrounding Stanley Plaza and **Murray House**, built in 1843 for the British Army and relocated stone by stone in 1982 from its previous site in Central, where the Bank of China now stands.

To the east, Stanley's touristy **market** (daily 10am–7pm) straddles the streets and alleys around Stanley Market Street, and is a good place to pick up clothing, bright tack and souvenirs. More impressive is the small **Tin Hau Temple** on the western side of the peninsula, dating from 1767. Typically, Tin Hau's statue has to share the hall with a dozen other deities of Taoist, Buddhist and local origins, along with a darkened tiger pelt, bagged nearby in 1942 – the last ever shot in Hong Kong. There are also lanterns and model ships, reminding you of Tin Hau's role as protector of fishermen, though there's little fishing done from Stanley these days. Stanley's best stretch of sand is **St Stephen's Beach**, fifteen minutes south along the shore, with a short pier, watersports centre, barbecue pits, showers and decent swimming. On the headland above, **Stanley Prison** was notorious during World War II, when hundreds of civilians were interned here in dire conditions by the Japanese.

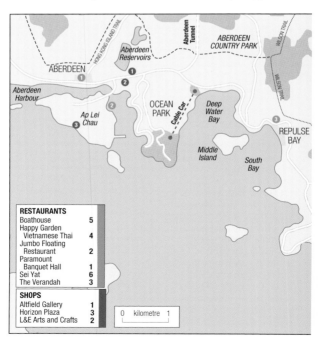

RESTAURANTS

Boathouse	5
Happy Garden Vietnamese Thai	4
Jumbo Floating Restaurant	2
Paramount Banquet Hall	1
Sei Yat	6
The Verandah	3

SHOPS

Altfield Gallery	1
Horizon Plaza	3
L&E Arts and Crafts	2

0   kilometre   1

DRAGON'S BACK HIKE TO SHEK O

THE DRAGON'S BACK

Bus #9 from Shau Kei Wan (next to the MTR station) or Shek O. MAP P.60-61
The Dragon's Back is the final section of the 50km-long **Hong Kong Island Trail**, which runs west to east across the island. Though the name sounds fierce, the two-hour hike is not too difficult, and at weekends you're likely to find plenty of other people tackling it. Conditions are exposed and can be hot, however, so take water and a hat.

Get off the bus at the **To Tei Wan Tsuen** stop, where there's a roadside parking bay and a map of the route, then follow the track up through woodland and scrub out onto the Dragon's Back itself.

This ridge runs north past granite outcrops, taking in views of Stanley town, green hills and fantastic seascapes, before skirting the rear of Mount Collison and descending to **Big Wave Bay**'s beaches. From here, it's a half-hour stroll south to Shek O.

HONG KONG ISLAND TRAIL

DRAGON'S BACK

▲ Mt Collinson (347m)

Big Wave Bay

TAI TAM COUNTRY PARK

Tai Tam Reservoir

SHEK O COUNTRY PARK

Rocky Bay

④ ● Shek O

Turtle Cove

★ To Tei Wan Tsuen Bus stop

STANLEY

⑤⑥

Tai Tam Bay

Stanley Bay

Cape D'Aguilar

Ferry to Po Toi Island

N

Hong Kong Island: the south side

SHEK O

Bus #9 from Shau Kei Wan (next to the MTR station); or Sun only #309 from Exchange Square, Central (hourly 2.10–6.10pm; last bus back departs Shek O at 7pm). MAP P.60–61

Shek O is an unpretentious village down at Hong Kong's southeastern reaches, with the best beach on the island. Wide, with white sand and fringed by shady trees, it can get very full at the weekend. There are also a few restaurants and expat bars in the village, and on Sunday extra snack stalls open, serving the crowds who come down to swim. Unsurprisingly, Shek O is one of the most desirable addresses in Hong Kong, and there are some upmarket pieces of real estate in the area. You can get a flavour of things by walking through the village parallel with the beach and following the path up to **Shek O Headland** for some sweeping panoramas.

For more space and fewer people, **Big Wave Bay** is a half-hour walk north of Shek O, with another good beach, barbecue pits and a refreshment kiosk.

Shopping

ALTFIELD GALLERY

9th Floor, Gee Chang Hong Centre, 65 Wong Chuk Hang Rd, Aberdeen. Call first ☎ 2552 1968. MAP P.60–61

Quality antiques from a dealer specializing in China and Southeast Asia. Everything from statues and maps to jewellery, but none of it a bargain.

HORIZON PLAZA

2 Lee Wing St, Ap Lei Chau island. Daily 10am–7pm. MAP P.60–61

28 storeys of discount furnishings and designer fashion labels – Hong Kong's major upmarket clothing stores, such as Joyce Boutique (21/F), send all last season's stock here. Also try the Beijing Antiques Shop (20/F) and Oriental Rugs (12/F).

L&E ARTS AND CRAFTS

11A Kwai Bo Industrial Building, 40 Wong Chuk Hang Rd, Aberdeen. Call first ☎ 2546 9886. MAP P.60–61

Stalwart of antique – and antique-style – home furnishings; a great place for a browse.

Restaurants

BOATHOUSE

88 Stanley Main St, Stanley ☎ 2813 4467. Mon–Fri 11.30am–10.30pm, Sat & Sun 11am–10.30pm. MAP P.60–61

Solid Brit-style pub food – steak, seafood platters, a bucket of prawns or plain fish and chips – served at pavement tables with sea views. A little bit pricey for what you get.

HAPPY GARDEN

Near the bus stop, Shek O ☎ 2809 4165. Daily noon–10pm. MAP P.60–61

One of several laidback places with outdoor tables, luridly coloured drinks and excellent food – try the water spinach with *belechan* beef, or huge Thai fish cakes. Mains cost around $100.

JUMBO FLOATING RESTAURANT

Shum Wan Pier Drive, Wong Chuk Hang. Bus #75 from Exchange Square, Central, to Shum Wan Pier, then take an on-demand ferry; restaurant pays the homeward taxi fare if you spend enough on your meal. ☎ 2553 9111. Mon–Sat 11am–11.30pm, Sun 9am–11.30pm. MAP P.60–61

A Hong Kong institution, this ridiculously ostentatious mess of golden dragons, florid rooflines and auspicious red decor is best seen at night, lit up like a Christmas tree. Their Cantonese food is competent rather than memorable, but set menus are not too expensive and it's fun as a one-off experience. The upper-storey Top Deck does indulgent champagne Sunday lunch buffets from 11.30am.

PARAMOUNT BANQUET HALL

Shop F, 1/F, Phase 5, Aberdeen Centre, Hoi Lung Court, Nam Ning St. ☎ 2884 9088. Daily 6am–midnight. MAP P.60–61

Huge, bright, noisy mid-range

JUMBO FLOATING RESTAURANT

place to wolf down an excellent *dim sum* breakfast; just watch out for the over-active air-conditioning. Above average seafood and roast meats.

SEI YAT

Stanley Market, Stanley ☎ 2813 0503. Daily noon–11pm. MAP P.60–61

No English sign for this legendary hole-in-the-wall, serving Hong Kong style French toast, milk tea and beef-and-egg sandwiches – local snacks rarely served up elsewhere these days.

THE VERANDAH

109 Repulse Bay Rd, Repulse Bay ☎ 2292 2822. Wed–Sat noon–10.30pm, Sun 11am–2.30pm. MAP P.60–61

Famous for its lavish Sunday brunches, afternoon teas and candle-lit dinners, this elegant establishment features colonial ambience in the dark wooden furniture, shutters and long sea views from the shaded balcony. Don't miss their Grand Marnier soufflé or the oysters.

Kowloon: Tsim Sha Tsui

Kowloon, from the Cantonese *gau lung* ("nine dragons", after an undulating ridge of hills here), was a twelve-square-kilometre peninsula on the Chinese mainland north of Hong Kong Island when the British seized it in 1860. Land reclamation has since more than doubled its size and Kowloon has become the most densely populated place on earth, nowhere more obvious than in the frenetic waterfront district of Tsim Sha Tsui, where many visitors stay, eat and – especially – shop. The quantity and variety of goods on sale here is staggering, and a devoted window-shopper can find every bauble, electronic gadget and designer label known to man. If it all sounds too gruesomely commercial, there's solace in the Cultural Centre and several museums, while Tsim Sha Tsui's waterfront provides one of the best views of Central's skyline.

THE WESTERN WATERFRONT

Ⓜ Tsim Sha Tsui, Exit J6. MAP P.65, POCKET MAP A18–C18

Tsim Sha Tsui's Star Ferry Pier is sited at Kowloon's southwestern tip; immediately outside is a 45m-high clocktower, dating from 1921, the only remnant of the grand train station which once welcomed European rail services. The ferry terminal sits at the bottom of a series of interconnected, upmarket shopping malls running up the western side of Tsim Sha Tsui's waterfront. The first section, **Ocean Terminal**, is where cruise liners dock, while the next two blocks up – **Ocean Centre** and **Harbour City** – between them form a maze of galleries, hotels, restaurants and pricey boutiques. At the far end, the **China Ferry Terminal** comprises another block of stores where ferries depart for China and Macau.

About a kilometre northwest of the Ferry Terminal, **ICC** – the International Commerce Centre – is Hong Kong's tallest building at 484m, and sits over Kowloon's Airport Express station.

THE PENINSULA HOTEL

Salisbury Rd Ⓜ Tsim Sha Tsui, Exit J6 ☎ 2920 2888, Ⓦ peninsula.com. MAP P.65, POCKET MAP B18

The *Peninsula Hotel* is one of Tsim Sha Tsui's few throwbacks to colonial times. Built in the 1920s next to the train station, the hotel offered a shot of elegance to Hong Kong's weary new arrivals who had spent weeks crossing Europe, Russia and China. It remains one of the most expensive and stylish addresses in Hong Kong, and still offers a taste of more refined times in its opulent lobby, where afternoon tea is served (daily 2–6pm, $358 per person); you don't have to be an overnight guest to dine, but note that dress rules apply (see box, p.67).

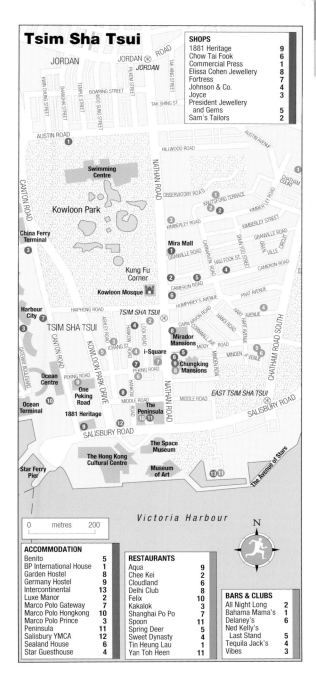

Tsim Sha Tsui

Victoria Harbour

0 metres 200

N

THE HONG KONG CULTURAL CENTRE

Salisbury Rd Ⓜ Tsim Sha Tsui, Exit J4 ☎ 2734 2009, Ⓦ lcsd.gov.hk/hkcc. Box office daily 9am–9pm. MAP P.65, POCKET MAP A18

The Hong Kong Cultural Centre was built in 1980 to provide a cultural hub for this otherwise overtly materialistic city. It contains a concert hall and several theatres, where events from classical Italian and Chinese opera through to contemporary dance are performed (contact the box office for current programmes). Worthy though all this is, the building itself proves that you need vision to create impressive architecture: astonishingly, given the dramatic harbourside location, the building has no windows. The pink-tiled exterior is awkwardly shaped, with angled walls and outshooting ribs creating a cloister surrounded by a starkly paved area, dotted with palm trees. An adjacent two-tiered walkway along the water offers the view of the harbour and Hong Kong Island denied from the inside; come here at night to see Central's towers in all their chromatic glory.

MUSEUM OF ART

10 Salisbury Rd Ⓜ Tsim Sha Tsui, Exit J4 Ⓦ hk.art.museum. Closed for renovation until 2018; check website for temporary exhibitions from the collection. MAP P.65, POCKET MAP B18

Hong Kong's Museum of Art houses six galleries of mostly classical Chinese works, with frequent touring exhibitions, often featuring masterpieces from collections on the mainland and Taiwan.

The first-floor **Chinese Antiquities Gallery** has an ever-changing exhibition of gold, jade and bronzes, many dating back several thousand years to the semi-mythical Shang, Xia and Zhou dynasties. The second floor's **Xubaizhai Gallery** concentrates on silk scroll painting and calligraphy; it's the spirit of the brush-strokes, rather than the subject itself, which is most admired. The adjacent **Contemporary Art Gallery** features post-1950s work, but in so many styles and going in so many directions that it's hard to tell what is important and what is just whimsy.

There's another staid but informative **Antiquities Gallery** on the third floor, strong on pottery: Neolithic clay pots with black patterns; lively Han figurines and tomb models of houses and watchtowers; and designs that, artistically at least, peaked with the Tang's abstract colours and the Song's simplicity. Also on the third floor, the **Historical Pictures Gallery** has a rotating selection of paintings, drawings and prints that trace the eighteenth- and nineteenth-century development of Hong Kong, Macau and Guangzhou as trading centres, as seen by both Western and local artists. The museum ends on the fourth floor with the **Chinese**

EXHIBITS AT THE MUSEUM OF ART

Afternoon tea

Heading to a smart hotel for British-style afternoon tea is a Hong Kong institution. The *Peninsula* is the most magnificent and "traditional" option, but there's also the *InterContinental* (Salisbury Rd, Tsim Sha Tsui); the *Lobby Lounge* at the *Island Shangri-La* (Two Pacific Place, 88 Queensway, Central); the *Tiffin Lounge* at the *Grand Hyatt* (Harbour Rd, Wan Chai); and the *Mandarin Oriental* (Connaught Rd, Central). You'll pay upwards of $300 per person. **Dress code** is "smart casual", ruling out shorts, sportswear, sandals, flip-flops and blue jeans.

AFTERNOON TEA AT THE PENINSULA

Fine Art Gallery, which shows exhibits from a collection of three thousand works, including modern Chinese art, and animal and bird paintings.

THE SPACE MUSEUM

Salisbury Rd Ⓜ Tsim Sha Tsui, Exit J4
☎ 2721 0226, ⓦ hk.space.museum. CLosed until late 2016 for renovation; check website for details. MAP P.65, POCKET MAP B18

The Chinese were the first to record Halley's Comet and the first to chart star movements – the Space Museum traces these breakthroughs and the entire history of astronomy with hands-on displays, push-button exhibits, video presentations and picture boards. There's also a **Space Theatre**, where an ever-changing selection of films (either on space or the natural world) is shown on the massive wraparound Omnimax screen, providing a thrilling sensory experience.

THE AVENUE OF STARS

Salisbury Rd Ⓜ Tsim Sha Tsui, Exit J4.
MAP P.65, POCKET MAP C18

Hong Kong's film industry is the third-largest in the world, despite production dropping off in recent years. This waterfront promenade east from the Space Museum celebrates its heroes with handprints and brass name plaques set in the pavement to luminaries such as Jackie Chan, Chow Yun Fat, Maggie Cheung, Wong Kar Wai and Raymond Chow. The biggest draw, however, is the **statue of Bruce Lee**, who catapulted the industry – and Chinese kung fu – to world attention in the 1970s; watch young Chinese striking a pose alongside for photos. The Avenue is also a great place to catch the nightly **Symphony of Lights** (8pm; free), when Central's coloured skyscrapers pulse and flash to a synthesized beat.

NATHAN ROAD

Ⓜ Tsim Sha Tsui. MAP P.65, POCKET MAP A10–B18

Nathan Road is Tsim Sha Tsui's – and Kowloon's – main thoroughfare, running north for 3km from the waterfront to Boundary Street. It's always packed, the pavements with extraordinarily thick crowds, and the roads with fast-moving traffic. It's not just the neon along here that glitters, but the shop windows too, full of jewellery, the latest cameras and mobile phones, clothes, shoes and fine art. Even window-shopping is a struggle nonetheless, what with the crowds, hustlers and the insistent hawkers.

Nathan Road has its own **shopping centres**, the most notorious of which are the seething downmarket complexes of Chungking Mansions (nos. 36–44) and Mirador Mansions (nos. 56–58), full of guesthouses, Indian restaurants and super-cheap stalls for daily necessities. Side streets are also alive with similar possibilities. To the east of Nathan Road, **Granville Road** is famous for its bargain clothes shops, some of them showcasing the work of new, young designers, though you'll also find clothing, accessory and jewellery stores all the way along Carnarvon, Cameron and Kimberley roads.

HONG KONG HISTORY MUSEUM

Chatham Rd South Ⓜ Tsim Sha Tsui, Exit B2/Hung Hom, Exit D6 Ⓦ hk.history.museum. Mon & Wed–Fri 10am–6pm, Sat & Sun 10am–7pm. $10, Wed free. POCKET MAP C16

The Hong Kong History Museum is an ambitious trawl through the region's past, using videos, light shows, interactive software and life-sized reconstructions. Things kick off with rainforest, which covered the island millions of years ago, then human development from the stone age, via early contact with mainland China during the Han dynasty, through to scale models of wooden junks that filled Hong Kong harbour until recent times, and a reproduction of a 1930s street complete with tea shops that smell of tea. Perhaps what's most striking is that these shops don't look much different from those in business in Mong Kok and Sheung Wan today, almost a hundred years later.

HONG KONG SCIENCE MUSEUM

Chatham Rd South Ⓜ Tsim Sha Tsui, Exit B2/Hung Hom, Exit D6 Ⓦ hk.science .museum. Mon & Wed–Fri 10am–7pm, Sat & Sun 10am–9pm. $10, Wed free. POCKET MAP C16

With four floors full of things to prod, pull and take to pieces, the Hong Kong Science Museum is really somewhere to bring children for a couple of hours – especially if it's raining. Each level has themed exhibitions exploring electricity, optical illusions, engineering (a very Hong Kong topic) and the like, in fun, hands-on ways. The seemingly easy 3D puzzles will keep even the adults busy for a while,

NEON SIGNS ON NATHAN ROAD

China's martial arts

China's many martial arts mostly trace their origins back to Henan province's Shaolin Temple, where, according to legend, the sixth-century monk Bodhidharma developed exercises to balance the inactivity of meditation. These evolved into fighting routines for defending the temple, and were gradually disseminated into the rest of China.

Early morning is the best time to catch people training – Kowloon and Victoria parks are especially popular. The large groups moving slowly through their routines are doing tai chi; specifically local styles include *wing chun* – which became famous as being the first martial art Bruce Lee studied – and *hung gar*, associated with the nineteenth-century master Wong Fei Hung.

TAI CHI IN KOWLOON PARK

while the Energy Machine features wooden balls racing around the entire museum along a giant maze of tracks, buckets, pulleys, drums and gongs – ask at the desk for performance times.

KOWLOON PARK

Ⓜ Tsim Sha Tsui, Exit A1. Daily 5am–midnight. MAP P.65, POCKET MAP A16–A17

Find an escape from the teeming masses in Kowloon Park, which stretches along Nathan Road between Haiphong and Austin roads. Parts of it have been landscaped and styled as a Chinese garden with fountains, rest areas, a children's playground, and two bird collections – the wildfowl (including flamingos and mandarin ducks) outside in landscaped ponds, the parrots and other exotically coloured

rainforest species contained in a small aviary. There's also a swimming complex (daily 6.30am–noon, 1–5pm & 6–10pm; $19) and a sculpture walk.

The southeastern corner of the park is taken up with an open area known as the **Kung Fu Corner**. Full of practitioners from about 6am every morning, it also hosts free displays of various martial arts between 2.30pm and 4.30pm every Sunday. Below it, at 105 Nathan Road, is the large **Kowloon Mosque** (no public access), built in the mid-1980s to replace a mosque originally built in 1894 for the British Army's Muslim troops from India. Leave the park at the southern end and you can drop down to Haiphong Road and its small covered produce market at the Canton Road end (daily 6am–8pm).

69

Shops

1881 HERITAGE

East of Canton Rd, between Salisbury & Peking roads Ⓜ Tsim Sha Tsui, Exit I3. MAP P.65, POCKET MAP A18

Ludicrous outdoor shopping mall on the site of the former Marine Police Station, brimming with upmarket boutiques – look for the giant floral teacup and pot.

CHOW TAI FOOK

63 Nathan Rd Ⓜ Tsim Sha Tsui, Exit D1. MAP P.65, POCKET MAP B17

Chain with a wide range of gold, diamond and jade jewellery at mid-range prices – a good place to get a feel for local styles and costs.

TAILORING SHOP

COMMERCIAL PRESS

Mira Mall basement, 118–130 Nathan Rd Ⓜ Tsim Sha Tsui, Exit B1. MAP P.65, POCKET MAP B17

Bright, modern bookshop with a broad range of photo-heavy coffee-table works and local literature in English, plus a great selection of Chinese-language titles.

ELISSA COHEN JEWELLERY

209 Hankow Centre, 5–15 Hankow Rd Ⓜ Tsim Sha Tsui, Exit L3. MAP P.65, POCKET MAP B18

Individual designs, either new or based on antique European or Chinese styles. Very elegant, though they tend to overdo things slightly with encrusting gems.

FORTRESS

4–6 Hankow Rd Ⓜ Tsim Sha Tsui, Exit L3. MAP P.65, POCKET MAP B17

A local electronics chain selling the latest mobiles, MP3 players, digital cameras and laptops. No bargains, but you won't get ripped off either; a good indicator of what to pay locally.

JOHNSON & CO.

44 Hankow Rd Ⓜ Tsim Sha Tsui, Exit A1. MAP P.65, POCKET MAP B17

Tailoring for mostly male customers (they were a favourite with British military personnel stationed in Hong Kong), this shop also deals in middle-of-the-road jewellery and watches.

Tailors and suits

As you'll realize after being harassed by touts every few paces along Nathan Road, Tsim Sha Tsui hosts an abundance of tailors specializing in making suits for visitors. Many produce excellent work, but bear a few things in mind: suits made in 24 hours tend to fall apart just as quickly (three days is a realistic minimum, and should involve a couple of fittings); prices for good work are good value but not cheap (expect to pay about the same as an off-the-peg suit at home); and you'll usually have to pay half the cost up front as a deposit.

JOYCE

G106 Gateway Arcade, Harbour City,
Canton Rd Ⓜ Tsim Sha Tsui, Exit C1.
MAP P.65, POCKET MAP A17

Hong Kong's most fashionable
boutique offers its own range of
clothing, as well as many top
overseas designer brands.

PRESIDENT JEWELLERY AND GEMS

Shop G16, *Holiday Inn* Golden Mile Mall,
50 Nathan Rd Ⓜ Tsim Sha Tsui, Exit D1.
MAP P.65, POCKET MAP B17

A small, family-run business
specializing in pearls and
diamonds, that also gives good
advice on buying high-quality
jewellery in Hong Kong
without getting ripped off.

SAM'S TAILORS

Burlington Arcade, 90–94 Nathan Rd Ⓜ Tsim
Sha Tsui, Exit B1. MAP P.65, POCKET MAP B17

A Hong Kong institution, as
much for Sam's talent for
self-publicity as for the quality
of his clothes – he's reputed to
have made suits for Bill Clinton,
Jude Law and Pierce Brosnan.

Restaurants

AQUA

29/F Penthouse, One Peking Rd Ⓜ Tsim Sha
Tsui, Exit E ☎ 3427 2288. Daily noon–2.30pm
& 6–11pm. MAP P.65, POCKET MAP A19

Enjoy superlative harbour
views from the sunken slate
tables as you consume an
unexpectedly successful blend
of Italian and Japanese dishes.
The atmosphere is informal,
and the prices high – at least
$480 a head.

CHEE KEI

37 Lock Rd Ⓜ Tsim Sha Tsui, Exit A1
☎ 2368 2528. Daily 11am–11pm. MAP P.65,
POCKET MAP B17

Bright Chinese diner serving
unpretentious, good-quality

JADE BRACELETS ON DISPLAY

wonton and noodle soups, fried
pork steak, crispy prawn rolls
and fishballs.

CLOUDLAND

Wah Fung Building, 17–23 Minden Ave
Ⓜ Tsim Sha Tsui, Exit D2 ☎ 2722 0156.
Daily 11am–11pm. MAP P.65, POCKET MAP C17

One of the most crowded
dim sum places in Kowloon,
with some unusual dishes
(caterpiller fungus beef
rolls) among a run of tasty
stalwarts: crispy pork,
seafood *congee*, prawn
dumplings and even fried rice.
Nice presentation too; around
$200 a head.

DELHI CLUB

Block C, 3/F, Chungking Mansions, 38–44
Nathan Rd Ⓜ Tsim Sha Tsui, Exit E
☎ 2368 1682. Daily noon–3.30pm &
6–11.30pm. MAP P.65, POCKET MAP B17

A Nepali curry house with
spartan surroundings,
slap-down service, and an
inexpensive set meal that
would feed an army. Also
recommended for their
vegetarian dishes, mutton
and tandoori specialities,
and clay-oven-cooked naan.

KAKALOK

FELIX

28/F, *Peninsula Hotel*, Salisbury Rd Ⓜ Tsim Sha Tsui, Exit E ☎ 2315 3188. Restaurant daily 6–10.30pm; bar daily 5pm–1.30am. Dress code. MAP P.65, POCKET MAP B18

Architect-designed restaurant with incredible views of Hong Kong Island (especially from the gents') which alone warrant a visit. The menu is not as good as it should be at over $650 a head, but many people just come for a Martini at the bar.

KAKALOK

Corner of Ashley Rd and Ichang St Ⓜ Tsim Sha Tsui, Exit A. ☎ 2376 1198. MAP P.65, POCKET MAP A17

Legendary hole-in-the-wall fast-food counter which serves the cheapest fish and chips in Hong Kong – their fried noodles aren't bad either. No seats, but Kowloon Park is 100m north.

SHANGHAI PO PO 336

6th Floor, i-Square, 63 Nathan Rd Ⓜ Tsim Sha Tsui, Exit C1 ☎ 2806 1833. Daily 8am–2am. MAP P.65, POCKET MAP B17

Popular, modern Shanghai restaurant, with a vast menu of moderately priced classic dishes like *xiaolongbao* dumplings and drunken chicken. Around $200 a head.

SPOON

Intercontinental Hotel, 18 Salisbury Rd Ⓜ East Tsim Sha Tsui, Exit J2 ☎ 2313 2323. Tues–Sat 6–11pm, Sun noon–2.30pm & 6–11pm. MAP P.65, POCKET MAP B18

You'll either love or hate this expensive, cutting-edge French restaurant: they serve some intriguing dishes, with an unusual blend of cooking styles, ingredients and sauces used in each. Over $600 a head.

SPRING DEER

1/F, 42 Mody Rd Ⓜ Tsim Sha Tsui, Exit D1 ☎ 2366 4012. Daily noon–2pm & 6–11.30pm. MAP P.65, POCKET MAP C17

Good-value place noted for its lack of decor, moderate prices and barrage of northern-Chinese favourites, such as Peking duck, baked fish on a hot plate, smoked chicken, and bean curd with minced pork. Around $200 per person.

SWEET DYNASTY

Pacific Centre, 28 Hankow Rd Ⓜ Tsim Sha Tsui, Exit F ☎ 2199 7799. Mon–Fri 8am–midnight, Sat & Sun 7.30am–midnight. MAP P.65, POCKET MAP B17

Casual but smart *dim sum* restaurant specializing in Southeast Asian desserts – lots of sticky rice, coconut milk, mango puddings and sago. A bit expensive, but fun.

TIN HEUNG LAU

18C Austin Avenue Ⓜ Jordan, Exit D ☎ 2366 2414. Daily noon–2.30pm & 6–10pm. MAP P.65, POCKET MAP C16

Not signed in English – look for the gold writing over the doorway. Unpretentious but expensive Shanghainese restaurant, whose signature dish is beggars' chicken ($400 a head; order in advance), baked in a clay casing which is smashed open at the table.

YAN TOH HEEN

Intercontinental Hotel, 18 Salisbury Rd
Ⓜ East Tsim Tsui, Exit J2 ☎ 2313 2323.
Mon–Sat noon–2.30pm & 6–11pm, Sun
11.30am–3pm & 6–11pm. MAP P.65,
POCKET MAP B18

Regarded as one of Hong
Kong's best for cutting-edge
Cantonese cooking – and for
the excellent service and
harbour views. Count on $250
a head for *dim sum*, or $2088
for the set menu.

Bars and clubs

ALL NIGHT LONG

9 Knutsford Terrace Ⓜ Tsim Sha Tsui, Exit
B1. Daily 5pm–4am. MAP P.65, POCKET MAP B16

Local version of Lan Kwai Fong's
Insomnia bar, with DJs and no
fewer than eight in-house bands
playing a mix of cheesy, jazzy
and contemporary sounds to a
lively yuppie audience. Feels
more spacious than it is thanks
to the open front.

BAHAMA MAMA'S

4–5 Knutsford Terrace Ⓜ Tsim Sha Tsui, Exit
B1. Mon–Thurs 5pm–3am, Fri & Sat 5pm–4am,
Sun 6pm–2am. MAP P.65, POCKET MAP B16

The beach-bar theme and
outdoor terrace attracts a party
crowd. For the best experience,
stump up the cover charge and
come along on club nights,
where a mixed-music policy
offers everything from garage
to world.

DELANEY'S

71–77 Peking Rd Ⓜ Tsim Sha Tsui, Exit E.
Daily 8am–2am. MAP P.65, POCKET MAP B17

Large basement bar with the
usual decor, Irish beer and pub
food, that somehow manages to
be more fun than most. Good
for a reasonably quiet drink
early on, though heats up
through the night.

NED KELLY'S LAST STAND

11A Ashley Rd Ⓜ Tsim Sha Tsui, Exit E. Daily
11.45am–1.45am. MAP P.65, POCKET MAP A17

Australian bar with good beer
and meaty Aussie food, plus
great live jazz after 9pm. A real
favourite with travellers.

TEQUILA JACK'S

35 Chatham Rd South Ⓜ Tsim Sha Tsui, Exit
D2. Daily noon till late. MAP P.65, POCKET MAP C17

Small Mexican-style watering
hole offering a bar list of
margaritas and imported beers,
plus Tex-Mex chow, a long bar
and pavement tables.

VIBES

5/F, The Mira Hong Kong, 118 Nathan Rd
Ⓜ Tsim Sha Tsui, Exit B1 ☎ 2315 5999.
Daily noon–4am, happy hour daily noon–10pm.
MAP P.65, POCKET MAP B16

Fifth-floor courtyard
lounge-bar open to the sky;
good for an evening cocktail
with chilled-jazz ambience.

BAND AT NED KELLY'S LAST STAND

Kowloon: Jordan to Diamond Hill

Kowloon's crowds and shopping ethos continue north of Tsim Sha Tsui into Jordan, Yau Ma Tei and Mong Kok. It's a great area for specialist street markets, most of them – once you get past touristy Temple Street Night Market – very Chinese in theme, with food, jade, pets, flowers and clothes on sale. You can also buy electronic goods at lower prices than in Tsim Sha Tsui, and with less chance of being ripped off.

Until the acquisition of the New Territories in 1898, Kowloon ended beyond Mong Kok at Boundary Street, though today it extends a further 3km north to a natural dividing line at the base of the jagged Kowloon Hills. This area beyond Boundary Street is largely residential, with a handful more markets and sights accessible by public transport – including a beautiful traditional garden at Diamond Hill.

VIEW DOWN SHANGHAI STREET

SHANGHAI AND RECLAMATION STREETS

Ⓜ Yau Ma Tei, Exit B2. MAP P.76-77, POCKET MAP A11-A15

The streets north of Jordan Road are interesting places to browse the low-key businesses which serve locals' daily needs. **Shanghai Street** contains an eclectic and attractive mix of shops and stalls selling items as diverse as bright-red Chinese wedding gowns (at no. 194), embroidered pillow cases, lacquered shrines and other temple accessories (at no. 216), chopping blocks, incense and kitchenware (including a smith selling razor-sharp cleavers at no. 297). To the west, **Reclamation Street** sports an intense produce market between Nanking and Kansu streets, offering concrete proof that the Cantonese demand absolutely fresh food, with fish, frogs and turtles alive in tanks and buckets for shoppers to inspect.

TEMPLE STREET NIGHT MARKET

Temple St, Jordan/Yau Ma Tei Ⓜ Jordan. Daily 5–11pm. MAP P.76–77, POCKET MAP A14–A15

Temple Street Night Market is crammed with stalls selling tourist-oriented clothes (for men particularly), Bruce Lee dolls and electrical knick-knacks, household goods, watches, posters and jewellery. Fortune-tellers and herbalists set up stalls in the surrounding streets and, if you're lucky, there'll be impromptu performances of Cantonese opera. About halfway up the street you'll see an undercover area of alfresco **seafood restaurants**: a couple of plates of sea snails, prawns, mussels or clams, with a beer or two, won't be expensive (fish often is though – fix all prices in advance), and it's a great place to stop for a while and take in the atmosphere. Some of the stalls even have formal English menus, if you want to know exactly what you're getting. In the middle of Temple Street is the heavy stone **Tin Hau Temple** itself (daily 8am–5pm; free), dedicated to the southern Chinese sea goddess – and indicating that this was once the local waterfront in the days before land reclamation. Note that the night market continues north from here along Temple Street.

THE JADE MARKET

Kansu St, Yau Ma Tei Ⓜ Yau Ma Tei, Exit C. Daily 9am–6pm. MAP P.76–77, POCKET MAP A14

Located under a busy overpass, Yau Ma Tei's Jade Market features several hundred stalls selling an enormous selection of jade jewellery, statues and antique reproductions. In part,

TIN HAU TEMPLE, TEMPLE STREET

jade owes its value to the fact that it's a hard stone and very difficult to carve; it's also said by the Chinese to promote longevity and prevent decay (in ancient times royalty used to be buried in jade suits made of thousands of tiny tiles held together with gold wire).

There are basically two kinds of jade: nephrite (which can be varying shades of green), and the rarer jadeite, much of which comes from Burma and which can be all sorts of colours. A rough guide to quality is that the jade should be cold to the touch and with a pure colour that remains constant all the way through; coloured tinges or blemishes can reduce the value. However, unless you know your stuff, the scope for being misled is considerable, so it's more enjoyable to just poke around the stalls to see what turns up for a few dollars. Note that all the serious buying is over before lunch.

75

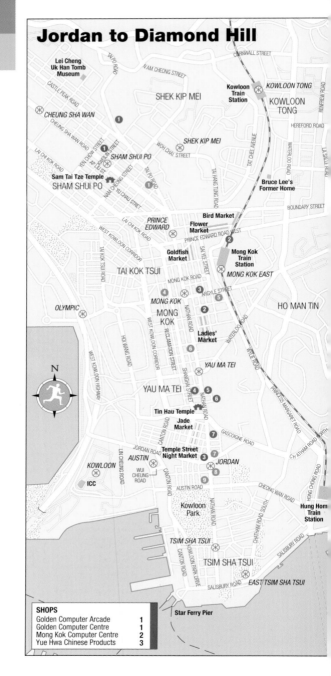

Jordan to Diamond Hill

CARNWALL STREET

Lei Cheng
Uk Han Tomb
Museum

TAI PO ROAD

N'AM CHEONG STREET

CASTLE PEAK ROAD

SHEK KIP MEI

Kowloon
Train
Station

KOWLOON TONG

**KOWLOON
TONG**

RENFREW ROAD

CHEUNG SHA WAN

CHEUNG SHA WAN ROAD

HEREFORD ROAD

WATERLOO ROAD

LA SALLE ROAD

SHEK KIP MEI
WOH CHAI STREET

TAT CHEE AVENUE

LAI CHI KOK RD

YEN CHOW STREET

AP LIU STREET

TAI PO ROAD

TAI HANG TUNG ROAD

Bruce Lee's
Former Home

Sam Tai Tze Temple

NAM CHEONG STREET

FU CHAU STREET

SHAM SHUI PO

BOUNDARY STREET

**PRINCE
EDWARD**

Bird Market
**Flower
Market**

PRINCE EDWARD ROAD WEST

LAI CHI KOK ROAD

WEST KOWLOON CORRIDOR

**Goldfish
Market**

SAI YEE STREET

**Mong Kok
Train
Station**

MONG KOK EAST

TAI KOK TSUI ROAD

TAI KOK TSUI

MONG KOK ROAD

MONG KOK

ARGYLE STREET

HO MAN TIN

OLYMPIC

WEST KOWLOON CORRIDOR

HOI WANG ROAD

NATHAN ROAD

**MONG
KOK**

RECLAMATION STREET

WATERLOO ROAD

WEST KOWLOON HIGHWAY

**Ladies'
Market**

YAU MA TEI

WYLIE ROAD

SHANGHAI STREET

YAU MA TEI

NATHAN ROAD

PRINCESS MARGARET ROAD

Tin Hau Temple
**Jade
Market**

**Temple Street
Night Market**

FERRY STREET

GASCOIGNE ROAD

CHATHAM ROAD NORTH

JORDAN

LIN CHEUNG ROAD

KOWLOON

ICC

JORDAN ROAD

WUI
CHEUNG
ROAD

CANTON ROAD

AUSTIN ROAD

AUSTIN

NATHAN ROAD

CHEONG WAN ROAD

HUNG HOM ROAD

**Kowloon
Park**

CHATHAM ROAD SOUTH

**Hung Hom
Train
Station**

TSIM SHA TSUI

CANTON ROAD

KOWLOON PARK DRIVE

SALISBURY ROAD

TSIM SHA TSUI

SALISBURY ROAD

EAST TSIM SHA TSUI

Star Ferry Pier

SHOPS	
Golden Computer Arcade	1
Golden Computer Centre	1
Mong Kok Computer Centre	2
Yue Hwa Chinese Products	3

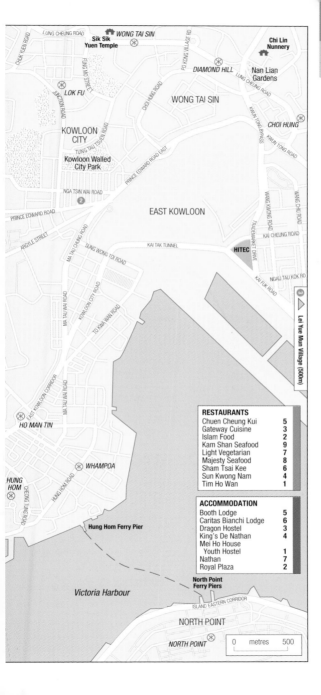

RESTAURANTS

Chuen Cheung Kui	5
Gateway Cuisine	3
Islam Food	2
Kam Shan Seafood	9
Light Vegetarian	7
Majesty Seafood	8
Sham Tsai Kee	6
Sun Kwong Nam	4
Tim Ho Wan	1

ACCOMMODATION

Booth Lodge	5
Caritas Bianchi Lodge	6
Dragon Hostel	3
King's De Nathan	4
Mei Ho House Youth Hostel	1
Nathan	7
Royal Plaza	2

THE LADIES' AND GOLDFISH MARKETS

Mong Kok Ⓜ Mong Kok, Exit D2. Daily from 10am till after 5pm. MAP P.76-77, POCKET MAP B12 & A10

Two more interesting markets can be found in Mong Kok's Tung Choi Street. Between Dundas and Shantung streets, the crowded stalls of the **Ladies' Market** mostly sell inexpensive clothing, though you might find better bargains at Sham Shui Po. North of Bute Street, the **Goldfish Market** is one long, crowded run of shops festooned with all kinds of ornamental and tropical fish in tanks and fairground-style plastic bags, as well as the necessary accessories for displaying them in the home. Goldfish are a popular symbol of good fortune and wealth in China (saying "gold fish" in Chinese sounds like saying "gold surplus") and are believed to invoke a trouble-free life; you'll often see drawings of fish or fish-shaped lanterns in temples or on display during Chinese festivals. Consequently, great care is taken with their breeding, and some can cost thousands of dollars.

THE FLOWER MARKET

Flower Market Rd, Mong Kok Ⓜ Prince Edward, Exit B1. Daily 10am–6pm. MAP P.76-77, POCKET MAP B10

North of Tung Choi Street and across busy Prince Edward Road, **Flower Market Road** hosts dozens of inexpensive florists and plant shops, best at the weekends when vendors bring in trucks full of orchids, orange trees and other exotica, crowding the narrow pavements with stalls. Chinese New Year is especially busy with people buying auspicious narcissi, orange trees and plum blossom to decorate their apartments.

DISPLAY AT THE GOLDFISH MARKET

THE BIRD MARKET

Off Prince Edward and Flower Market roads, Mong Kok Ⓜ Prince Edward, Exit B1. Daily 7am–8pm. MAP P.76-77, POCKET MAP B10

Mong Kok's Bird Market is housed in a purpose-built Chinese-style garden. There are two or three dozen stalls crammed with caged songbirds, parakeets, mynah birds, live crickets tied up in little plastic bags (they're fed to the birds with chopsticks), birdseed barrels and newly made bamboo cages – minus bird, these start at $100 or so. Little porcelain bird bowls and other paraphernalia cost from around $10. It's interesting just to watch the locals who bring their own caged birds here for an airing and to listen to them sing; taking your songbird out for a walk is a popular pastime among older Chinese men, one you'll see often in parks throughout more traditional areas of Hong Kong.

SHAM SHUI PO

Ⓜ Sham Shui Po. MAP P.76-77, POCKET MAP A10

Northwest of Boundary Street, shabby Sham Shui Po is full of **wholesale fashion warehouses** lining central Cheung Sha Wan Road for several blocks. Prices, styles and quantity here outdo Mong Kok's Ladies' Market, while surrounding streets stock haberdashery – fabrics, buttons, ribbon, lace – along with toys and handbags in leather and plastic.

South and parallel with Cheung Sha Wan Road, **Ap Liu Street flea market** (noon until after dark) is where to find all manner of junk and cheap household appliances, from secondhand cameras, power tools and mobile phones to old records from the 1930s, fishing rods and used furniture. As long as you don't expect to unearth anything valuable, it's good fun. The market extends south down Kweilin Street, where at no. 38D you'll find **Leung Choi Shun**, a family-run, traditional "bonesetting" apothecary founded a century ago.

Off Kweilin Street down Yu Chau Street, the **Sam Tai Tze Temple** (daily 8am–5pm) dates to the 1890s, built to house a statue of the unruly boy-god Na Cha – also known as Third Prince, or Sam Tai Tze – whom locals believed had subdued an outbreak of plague. Inside, Na Cha is depicted holding a sword, flanked by Pao Kung, the god of justice, and Kwun Yam, the goddess of mercy.

LEI CHENG UK HAN TOMB MUSEUM

41 Tonkin St, Cheung Sha Wan Ⓜ Cheung Sha Wan, Exit A3, then a 10min walk. ☎ 2386 2863. 10am–6pm, closed Thurs. Free. MAP P.76-77, POCKET MAP A10

Discovered in 1957 during construction of a housing estate, Lei Cheng Uk's cross-shaped burial chamber dates to the Eastern Han period (25–220 AD) and proves the region was even then under Chinese control. The museum shows an informative video outlining the excavation of the tomb and the culture that produced it; from here you pass cases of pottery and fragments of bronzeware unearthed at the site to reach the tomb itself, which has been preserved *in situ*. You can't go in, but a glass window gives you a peek at the low-ceilinged, interlocked brickwork. The tomb was presumably built for a local official, though no trace of a body was ever discovered.

KOWLOON WALLED CITY PARK

Tung Tau Tsuen Rd, Kowloon City. Bus #1 from the Tsim Sha Tsui Star Ferry Pier. Daily 6.30am–11pm. MAP P.76-77

After the British took Hong Kong Island in the 1840s, the Chinese government built a line of defences in what is now northern Kowloon, including a walled garrison town of about five hundred soldiers. When the New Territories were leased to Britain in 1898, the garrison commanders refused to cede sovereignty, and for the following century "**Kowloon Walled City**", as it became known, remained a self-governing enclave. In fact, the walls came down during World War II and were incorporated into a nearby airstrip, but during the late 1940s mainland Chinese refugees settled the area and built a high-rise shanty town, which became the haunt of Triad gangs and a no-go area for the police. It took until 1991 to negotiate the Walled City's closure, after which the site was levelled and turned into **Kowloon Walled City Park**. The restored *yamen* (former military headquarters) now houses a photo collection of the Walled City, though the only solid relics of the times are two stone blocks carved with the characters for "south gate", set into an ornamental wall.

LEI YUE MUN

Ⓜ Yau Tong, Exit A2, then a 10min walk.
MAP P76–77

Overlooking the eastern end of Victoria Harbour, **Lei Yue Mun** village is a ramshackle settlement of low plaster buildings, packed so close together that overhanging corrugated iron roofs turn its narrow lanes into tunnels. At the far side of the village, an ancient Tin Hau temple sits among some large granite boulders, where two rusting canons point south over the harbour's narrow neck towards the Museum of Coastal Defence.

Most people visit Lei Yue Mun to **eat seafood**, with the village's fresh-fish shops displaying tanks of live reef fish, clams, sea snails, crayfish, cuttlefish and shrimps. You make your choice from a shop, where it will be weighed and priced, then take it to a restaurant to have it cooked to your instructions. You pay all bills at the end, so watch out for scams: fix the price of your fish before it's bashed on the head, and the cost of cooking it before it gets handed to a chef. Restaurants do open for lunch, but evenings are the liveliest time to come.

SIK SIK YUEN TEMPLE

Lung Cheung Rd, Wong Tai Sin Ⓜ Wong Tai Sin, Exit B2. Daily 7am–5.30pm. Free.
MAP P76–77, POCKET MAP D10

The lavishly decorated Sik Sik Yuen Temple, built in 1921, is dedicated to **Wong Tai Sin** ("Yellow Immortal"), a shepherd during the Jin Dynasty (265–420 AD) who achieved enlightenment and became known for his healing powers. The temple is Hong Kong's major Taoist shrine, and some three million people visit annually to pay their respects, wish for long life and have their fortunes told. The temple's forecourt walls are lined with scores of fortune-tellers who read palms, bumps, feet and faces; some speak English and many display testimonials from satisfied customers.

The main temple building with its statue of Wong Tai Sin is often closed, but kneeling crowds perpetually pack out the front courtyard, burning incense and shaking pots full of numbered bamboo strips known as "fortune sticks". When one falls out it's exchanged for a piece of paper bearing the same number, which offers a prediction. The busiest days at the temple are around Chinese New Year and at Wong Tai Sin's festival, on the twenty-third day of the eighth lunar month (usually in Sept).

Behind the main building is the **Good Wish Garden** (Tues–Sun 9am–4pm; $2), with Chinese pavilions, carp ponds and waterfalls.

SHA TIN PASS

Sha Tin Pass Rd, Wong Tai Sin Ⓜ Wong Tai Sin, then green minibus #18 to Sha Tin Pass Rd. POCKET MAP C10

Sik Sik Yuen sits right up against the looming **Kowloon**

WORSHIPPERS AT SIK SIK YUEN TEMPLE

Hills, from where there are fantastic views south at the **Sha Tin Pass**. From the #18 bus stop, follow Sha Tin Pass Road uphill for a stiff, forty-minute ascent to the pass – popular with locals at the weekend – and once at the wooded top you'll find toilets, a pavilion and a small drinks kiosk (closes at 5pm).

Despite the name, the Sha Tin Pass – or the road, at any rate – doesn't run on to Sha Tin in the New Territories, though there is a footpath in that direction which lands you near Tsang Tai Uk (see p.89) in around another ninety minutes. There's also a marked 1.8km trail to Lion Rock from the top of Sha Tin Pass Road – see p.88 for more.

CHI LIN NUNNERY

Fun Tak Rd, Diamond Hill Ⓜ Diamond Hill, Exit C1, then a 5min walk. Daily 9am–4pm. Free. MAP P.76–77, POCKET MAP D10

Though only recently founded, Chi Lin Nunnery is, uniquely for Hong Kong, built in the ninth-century Tang style, with beautifully proportioned, dark timber buildings arranged around spacious central courtyards. Giant gilded representations of Buddha as the sage Sakyamuni, Manjusri (the incarnation of wisdom) and Samantabhadra (virtue) fill the main hall, whose roof sprouts two upright "horns", a structural necessity to give a gentle curve to the roofline. Side wings contain more statues of Buddhist deities in gold and precious wood – look for a languid one of Avalokitesvara, the original Indian source for Kwun Yam, the Chinese goddess of mercy. The temple is an extremely calming place to visit, joined by a footbridge to the equally tranquil Nan Lian Gardens.

NAN LIAN GARDENS

NAN LIAN GARDENS

Fun Tak Rd, Diamond Hill Ⓜ Diamond Hill, Exit C1 then a 5min walk. Daily 7am–9pm. Free. MAP P.76–77, POCKET MAP D10

Despite being sited in the middle of a ring of busy traffic overpasses, the **Nan Lian Gardens** form a delightful oasis. They're screened by trees which block the traffic noise and the sight of soaring apartment blocks outside, and once through the gates you may as well have stepped back over a thousand years into groves of contorted pine trees, dwarf bougainvillea and crepe myrtles, all laid out in the classical Chinese style. Large, oddly shaped rocks evoke landscapes in miniature, while ponds – one full of giant carp, another graced by a stunning gold-painted pavilion, reached via gently arched vermilion bridges – add a sense of space. Several wooden halls around the perimeter are also built to ancient designs; one contains a gift shop, another a gallery and the third displays models of the intricate wooden brackets that support the roofs. The gardens are not especially large, but the layout makes it feel bigger and it's easy to spend an hour strolling around here.

Shops

GOLDEN COMPUTER CENTRE & GOLDEN COMPUTER ARCADE

The entire block between Kweilin and Yen Chow streets, Sham Shui Po Ⓜ Sham Shui Po, Exit D2, ahead on the left. Daily 11am–8pm. MAP P.76–77, POCKET MAP A10

Cramped, crowded and mildly seedy palace of computer and electronics accessories on multiple floors. Prices here really are a good deal if you know what you're after, though once-plentiful software pirates have been raided out of business.

MONG KOK COMPUTER CENTRE

Nelson St, between Tung Choi and Fa Yuen streets, Mong Kok Ⓜ Mong Kok, Exit E2 and to the right. Daily 11am–8pm. MAP P.76–77, POCKET MAP B12

Similar to Sham Shui Po's Golden Computer Centre, though closer to the downtown area and without the range or bedrock prices. Still worth a browse if you're after inexpensive electronics and computer parts.

YUE HWA CHINESE PRODUCTS EMPORIUM

301–309 Nathan Rd, Jordan Ⓜ Jordan, Exit A. Daily 10am–10pm. MAP P.76–77, POCKET MAP B15

Longstanding department store specializing in Chinese souvenirs – everything from gift-wrapped medicines and tea to reproduction antique porcelain and massage chairs. Particularly good for clothing and trinkets.

Restaurants

CHUEN CHEUNG KUI

33 Nelson St, Mong Kok Ⓜ Mong Kok, Exit E2 ☎ 2396 0672. Daily 11am–11.45pm. MAP P.76–77, POCKET MAP B11

Hakka home-style cooking from China's Guangdong province – the salt-baked chicken, juicy and tender, is a house speciality. Moderate prices make this a popular place with locals, and there's also an English menu.

GATEWAY CUISINE

G/F 58A Praya Rd, Lei Yue Mun Ⓜ Yau Tong ☎ 2727 4628. Ⓦ gatewaycuisine.com /eng. Daily 11am–11pm. MAP P.76–77

The last restaurant at Lei Yue Mun, offering sea views and tasty seafood, including razor clams fried with black beans, steamed tiger prawns and soy-steamed scallops. A seven-dish meal costs around $350 a head.

ISLAM FOOD

1 Lung Kong Rd, Kowloon City ☎ 2382 2822. Daily 11am–11pm. MAP P.76–77

Down-to-earth food from northwestern China's Xinjiang province, where the people are mostly Muslim and the food distinctly central Asian. Plump for one of their juicy beef buns, flavoured with spring onion and wrapped in a crispy

DIM SUM AT MAJESTY SEAFOOD

coating, or "mutton curry" – a spicy lamb stew.

KAM SHAN SEAFOOD

7/F, Chuang's London Plaza, 219 Nathan Rd Ⓜ Jordan, Exit C1 ☎ 2376 3288. Daily 11am–4pm & 6pm–midnight. MAP P.76–77, POCKET MAP B16

Noisy, cheerful place serving excellent fried mantis shrimps, steamed mussels, crispy chilli whitebait, Cantonese roast goose, squid with garlic and crunchy-fried sweet noodles.

LIGHT VEGETARIAN

G/F, New Lucky House, 13 Jordan Rd Ⓜ Jordan, Exit B2 ☎ 2384 2833. Daily 11am–11pm. MAP P.76–77, POCKET MAP B15

Cantonese vegetarian fare, with everything made out of vegetables, gluten or tofu despite the names: sweet and sour "fish" (taro); a "bird's nest" basket with fried vegetables; and "duck" (marinated, fried beancurd skin packets). Can be overly stodgy if you order the wrong mix of dishes. Mains for around $75 a head.

MAJESTY SEAFOOD

3/F, Prudential Centre, 216–228 Nathan Rd, Jordan Ⓜ Jordan, Exit E ☎ 2723 2399. Daily 7.30am–10pm, *dim sum* until 1pm. MAP P.76–77, POCKET MAP B15

Ride the lift to the third floor and settle down, surrounded by fish tanks, for first-rate beef balls, leek dumplings, *char siu* puffs and egg custard tarts in this popular *dim sum* venue. Come prepared for arctic air-conditioning.

SHAM TSAI KEE

G/F, 99 Portland St, Yau Ma Tei Ⓜ Yau Ma Tei, Exit A1 ☎ 2780 3768. Daily noon–4.30pm. MAP P.76–77, POCKET MAP B15

Well-regarded *cha chaan teng* serving straightforward soup noodles, rice dishes and stir-fries. No English sign, and you might have to order

LIGHT VEGETARIAN

by pointing at what others are eating.

SUN KWONG NAM

631–633 Shanghai St, Mong Kok Ⓜ Mong Kok, Exit C2 ☎ 2395 0695. Daily 7am–9pm. MAP P.76–77, POCKET MAP A11

This Malay-Chinese *cha chaan teng* is a teahouse-cum-fast food joint full of locals, serving Malaysian curries, weird milky drinks with sago balls, baked pork chops in sweet and sour sauce and trademark Hong Kong "yin-yang coffee" – a mix of tea, coffee and condensed milk.

TIM HO WAN

9–11 Fuk Wing St, Sham Shui Po Ⓜ Sham Shui Po, Exit B2 ☎ 2788 1226. Mon–Fri 10am–10pm, Sat & Sun 9am–10pm. MAP P.76–77

Crowds queue round the block to eat at this apparently insignificant place, hungry for their Michelin-star-rated lotus-leaf steamed rice, *char siu* pastries, persimmon cakes and *fun gwor* dumplings. You may wait over an hour for a seat, so it's best to grab a ticket and go shopping.

The New Territories

The New Territories occupy 794 square kilometres between Kowloon and the Chinese border, home to just under half of Hong Kong's population. Here you'll find self-contained New Towns, built to ease Hong Kong's downtown population pressures, whose modern apartment blocks and shopping malls conceal nineteenth-century temples, fascinating museums, markets and traditional walled villages.

Away from these hubs the New Territories are essentially rural, with large parts designated as country parks, offering excellent hiking and coastal walks – especially around the easterly Sai Kung Peninsula. There are also some fun outdoor sights for children, notably the Hong Kong Wetland Park and Kadoorie Farm. With comprehensive rail and bus services, no single destination in the New Territories is beyond the reach of a day-trip from Hong Kong's downtown – which is fortunate, as there's little hotel accommodation out here.

SHING MUN COUNTRY PARK

3.5km east of Tsuen Wan Ⓜ Tsuen Wan, Exit B1, then green minibus #82 from Shiu Wo St to Pineapple Dam. MAP P.86–87

Shing Mun Country Park offers an easy two-hour walk around the deep blue waters of Shing Mun Reservoir (or Jubilee Reservoir). Choose a nice day, take a picnic and expect to see birds, reptiles and, almost certainly, **monkeys**.

The bus drops you outside the visitors' centre at the foot of Pineapple Dam, from where a

SHING MUN RESERVOIR

signposted circuit runs clockwise around the reservoir through the shady forest. The best picnic ground is about forty minutes along at the site of a village that was abandoned when the dam was built in 1928. The overgrown remains of rice-terrace walls can still be seen among the trees, though it's hard to imagine this once having been open hillside.

Past the briefly steep tail-end of the lake, the countryside opens up a little and finally reaches the reservoir's huge dam wall, set above a deep gorge. There's another picnic ground here with tables and benches, and it's just fifteen minutes back to the bus stop.

KAM TIN

Kam Sheung Rd Ⓜ Kam Sheung Road, Exit B and follow signposts for 5min. MAP P.86–87
Kam Tin township is famous for its outlying walled stone villages, the most visited of which is **Kat Hing Wai** (daily 9am–5pm; $1), which has been inhabited for four hundred years by the Tang clan. The village's iron gates were confiscated during resistance to the British takeover of the New Territories in 1898, and were returned in 1925 after being found in Ireland. Today, Kat Hing Wai is somewhat commercialized, and while the buildings inside the massive encircling wall are very ordinary, the atmosphere is a lifetime removed from Hong Kong's downtown.

About 600m north from here on Shui Tau Road, **Shui Tau Tsuen** village is bigger, and though the protective walls have gone there's a good scattering of old stone temples, narrow lanes and ancestral halls with elegantly carved roofs still standing amid the buildings of a more recent housing estate. Even the modern buildings here reflect the village's original fortified intent, presenting outsiders with security-grilled windows and stark tiled walls.

MACAQUE MONKEY, SHING MUN RESERVOIR

TAI MO SHAN

4km north of Tsuen Wan Ⓜ Tsuen Wan West, Exit D, then left to bus depot for bus #51 to the "Country Park" stop at Tsuen Kam Au. MAP P.86–87

Hong Kong's highest peak at 957m high, Tai Mo Shan is nonetheless easy to climb along a vehicle road all the way up the mountain's west face; people come here on cold winter mornings hoping to see frost. The top is often obscured by a smudge of cloud (*tai mo shan* means "Big Hat Mountain"), but on a good day you can see all the way to Lantau Island and the Chinese border. Note that the walk is very exposed, with no shade most of the way; if you want to catch the sunrise or sunset, consider staying overnight part way up at the basic *Sze Lok Yuen Youth Hostel* (see p.127).

From the **visitors' centre**, follow the picnic ground trail from the toilet block up steps through dry woodland on to a grassy hillside dotted with huge granite boulders. On the way you'll see docile wild cattle – the descendants of farmed herds – then the intermittent path joins the road near the youth hostel. Keep to the main road as it climbs, the scenery getting better with every bend, until you finally reach the summit area. A weather station prevents you from standing on the very top, but the views are just stupendous.

HONG KONG WETLAND PARK

Tin Shui Wai Ⓜ Tin Shui Wai, Exit E3 to Light Rail platform, then train #706 to Wetland Park Ⓦ wetlandpark.gov.hk. Daily except Tues 10am–5pm. $30. MAP P.86–87

Hong Kong Wetland Park covers over half a square

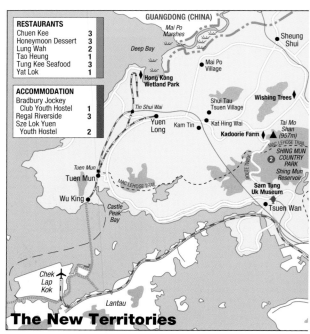

Hiking trail information

Hiking maps and information for all country parks and trails covered in this chapter can be found online at ⓦafcd.gov.hk, under "Country and Marine Parks". English-language bookshops also stock the pocket-sized *Hiker's Guide to Hong Kong*, with maps and trail accounts. Remoter country trails are not always well marked, and many are exposed, with little shade in summer, so wear a hat and take plenty of water.

kilometre of landscaped saltwater marsh along the Chinese border. The place is so busy with cheerful crowds that you're unlikely to see much wildlife, but it makes a wonderful half-day excursion if you have children to entertain. The park's paths weave over shallow ponds to **bird hides**, with telescopes trained over the mudflats. You'll see herons and egrets; in November, waders, ducks, camouflaged

snipe and – if you're lucky – rare black-faced spoonbills drop in. Other highlights include the mangrove boardwalk, where you can watch mudskippers and fiddler crabs, and the butterfly garden, full of bright flowers and pretty insects. Back inside, the **visitors' centre** has a glassed-in observation deck overlooking ponds, an aquarium with fish and crocodiles, and tanks full of insects and amphibians.

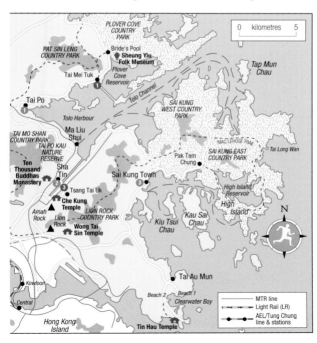

LION ROCK COUNTRY PARK

Access as for Sha Tin Pass (p.80); or Ⓜ Tai Wai, "Che Kung Miu" exit, then taxi 1km up Hung Mui Kuk Rd to park entrance. Free.
MAP P.86–87

Lion Rock Country Park covers a forested ridge at the western end of the Kowloon Hills which divide Kowloon from the New Territories. From the Tai Sin side, the trail first climbs in thirty minutes to **Amah Rock**, said to be a woman who turned to stone waiting for her husband to return from fishing.

Young women make the pilgrimage up here during the **Maidens' Festival**, held on the seventh day of the seventh lunar month (usually in Aug). From here, **Lion Rock** is a further hour's hike on a steadily rougher trail, culminating in an easy scramble up to two peaks formed by the lion's "head" and "rump" – on a clear day the views over Kowloon and the harbour are superb. Lion Rock is also a popular spot for **rock climbing**, the best source of information on which is Ⓦhongkongclimbing.com, which provides practical details for a score of routes in Hong Kong, and links to local clubs and climbing centres.

CHE KUNG TEMPLE

Ⓜ Che Kung Temple. Follow signs to the temple for 250m. Daily 9am–5pm. Free.
MAP P.86–87

The austere Che Kung Temple can be visited en route to Tsang Tai Uk village. Dedicated to the Song Dynasty general Che Kung, who is – among other duties – the god of gamblers, the black-roofed stone building dates to 1993, its entrance marked by a crowd of fortune-tellers, palm readers and incense sellers. Inside, beyond the courtyard, is a 10m-high, aggressive-looking statue of the general with a drawn sword and a collection of brass fans, which people turn for luck.

Che Kung's **festival** is held on the third day of Chinese New Year (in Jan or Feb), when – gambling being so important to the Chinese – the temple is heaving with people coming here to pray for good luck.

AMAH ROCK

TSANG TAI UK

Ⓜ Che Kung Temple. Follow signs to the village for 500m. Small donation expected.
MAP P.86–87

Tsang Tai Uk ("The Tsangs' Mansion") is one of the New Territories' lesser-touristed walled clan villages, built in the 1870s. Though it is somewhat dilapidated, a visit here provides an insight into how many of the New Territories' families used to live until skyscrapers and freeways began to dominate the area in the 1980s. Fortress-like clan villages are a **Hakka** speciality, as these people were dislodged hundreds of years ago by warfare in their homelands in central China, and have never been sure of their welcome in places they subsequently settled. Indeed, *hakka* translates as "guest family", indicating their perpetual status as outsiders.

A triple gateway leads into the village, which includes a

CHE KUNG TEMPLE

central courtyard, wide alleys, a network of high-ceilinged rooms and the clan ancestral hall. The most obvious traditional features are the **four watchtowers** at each corner of the outer wall, whose high, rounded eaves are adorned with spikes to keep bad luck away. The community is very much present, the village's alleyways choked with bicycles, gas canisters, discarded furniture and drying washing.

New Towns

In 1898, when the **New Territories** were first leased to Britain, fewer than ten thousand farmers and fishermen lived in the area. Today, the regional population stands at some 3.7 million, mostly housed in nine New Towns. Each **New Town** is designed to be self-sufficient, and for the majority they offer a better environment to live in than the crowded tenement slums of Mong Kok or the outer reaches of Kowloon. Although residential living space in the New Towns is similarly limited, more is provided here in the uncluttered layout of public amenities, civic and leisure services, shops, markets and transport infrastructure.

A look round a New Town gives an insight into the lives of many Hong Kong residents, and what civic planning can achieve in just a few years, given a coherent programme. **Sha Tin** is perhaps the most attractive example, since it's splendidly sited and has had time to acquire a certain character. **Tai Po** is another very liveable example, thanks to the successful blend of new amenities complementing an older, community-oriented town centre, though the New Town's designers don't always get things right: **Tin Shui Wai**, near the Wetland Park, is a horribly anonymous shell of concrete malls and blank-faced residential tower blocks, and has a sad reputation for depression and suicides.

TEN THOUSAND BUDDHAS MONASTERY

SHA TIN

Ⓜ Sha Tin. MAP P.86–87

Sha Tin – Sandy Fields – is a sprawling New Town development built either side of the Shing Mun River, home to more than half a million people. The town centre is covered by interconnected shopping complexes, of which the massive **New Town Plaza** is the biggest and busiest, packed with restaurants, good-value shops and cruising crowds. Outside, **Sha Tin Park** gives mild relief from the anodyne architecture, with bamboo gardens, a riverside walk and views east over the water to **Lion Rock Park** and Ma On Shan's distinctively hooked peak.

Aside from the Ten Thousand Buddhas Monastery (opposite), the town's best-known sight is the **Sha Tin Racecourse** (Ⓜ Racecourse, open race days only; Ⓦ sha-tin.com; $10), 3km northeast. It's Hong Kong's second racetrack after Happy Valley, and meetings are held on Wednesday evenings or Saturday and Sunday afternoons during the racing season (Sept–June).

The biggest annual event is the Hong Kong Derby in March, a 2km race for 4-year-olds, which attracts an international crowd.

HONG KONG HERITAGE MUSEUM

Man Lam Rd, Sha Tin Ⓜ Sha Tin/Che Kung Temple and follow signs Ⓦ www .heritagemuseum.gov.hk. Mon & Wed–Fri 10am–6pm, Sat, Sun & public hols 10am–7pm. $10, Wed free.

The Hong Kong Heritage Museum is the SAR's largest museum, though it's really of more interest for its temporary shows – which tend to showcase excellent and informative collections of Chinese art and historical artefacts – than its frankly lifeless permanent exhibitions. The best of these is the **Cantonese Opera Heritage Hall**, full of flamboyant costumes, embroidered shoes, stage props and mock-ups of traditional stage sets. The **Gallery of Chinese Art** features fine Chinese ceramics, bronze, jade, lacquerware and stone sculptures, while the **New Territories Heritage Hall** has archeological remains dating back to 4000 BC, accounts of Hong Kong's various Chinese ethnic groups, plus information about ancestral worship, feasts and festivals.

TEN THOUSAND BUDDHAS MONASTERY

Ⓜ Sha Tin; exit down the ramp, follow the road around to the left and take the first right to the end, where you'll find a sign and footpath for the monastery. Daily 10am–5pm. Free. MAP P.86–87

The recently renovated Ten Thousand Buddhas Monastery dates from the 1960s, and looks down over Sha Tin from Po Fook Hill. Four hundred steep steps ascend to the monastery from behind the Grand Central Plaza Shopping Centre, lined by five hundred life-sized, gilded statues of Buddhist saints. The main hall has an undistinguished exterior but houses thirteen thousand small black-and-gold Buddha statues, each sculpted in a different posture, lining the walls to a height of 10m or more. The building also contains the embalmed and gilded body of a monk, the founder of the monastery. Outside on the terrace there's a small pagoda, along with some brightly painted concrete statues of Chinese deities. **Vegetarian lunches** are also available, either from the menu or from a better-value canteen selection.

TAI PO

Ⓜ Tai Po Market. MAP P.86–87

The pleasant New Town of Tai Po, which faces east out to sea up the scenic Tolo Channel, is the jumping-off point for the Lam Tsuen Wishing Trees and countryside at Plover Cove (see p.92).

Tai Po is all about markets, so head to modern **Tai Po Hui Market** on Heung Sze Wui Street, a five-minute walk from Tai Po Market station. It's a frenetic mix of meat, seafood, vegetables and fruit, with a cooked food centre on the second floor serving inexpensive meals.

North of here, beyond On Fu Road, **Fu Shin Street** is a busy lane of open-air stalls piled with fresh produce, dried seafood and herbs. The granite **Man Mo Temple** halfway along, full of smoke, red brocade and carved wooden altars, was built to celebrate the market's foundation in 1892. Uphill at the southern end of On Fu Road, the **Hong Kong Railway Museum** (Mon & Wed–Sun 10am–6pm; free) occupies the unique Chinese-style old station, built in 1913, and is packed with wooden furnishings, model trains and photographs documenting the construction of the original Kowloon-to-Canton Railway. Out the back are coaches and engines from the 1920s to 1950s.

North of the Lam Tsuen River, the town's **Tin Hau Temple** (Ting Kok Road; free) was built around three hundred years ago and reflects Tai Po's former importance as a fishing centre. During the annual **Tin Hau festival** the temple is hung with coloured banners and ribbons, and Cantonese opera performances take place on a temporary stage over the road.

MARKET STREET IN TAI PO

TAI PO KAU NATURE RESERVE

Green minibus #28K from Kwong Fuk Rd in Tai Po, 2.5km southeast to park gates at Tsung Tsai Yuen bus stop. Daily 8am–5pm. Free. MAP P.86–87

Tai Po Kau Nature Reserve is a pleasant, thickly wooded area whose colour-coded walking trails take from thirty minutes to over three hours to complete. In the forest there are plenty of butterflies, monkeys and birdlife – especially **sunbirds** and **minivets**, otherwise rare in Hong Kong. Picnic sites at the reserve make this a nice place for an outdoor lunch.

KADOORIE FARM

Lam Kan Rd. Bus #64K from Ⓜ Tai Po Market or Kam Tin. Ⓦ kfbg.org.hk. Daily 9.30am–5pm; check opening hours online – it's closed for even minor holidays. $30. MAP P.86–87

A kilometre west of the Wishing Trees, Kadoorie Farm is a working farm specializing in organic and sustainable agriculture, beautifully located on the forested northern slopes of Tai Mo Shan (see p.86). Paths lead up through a forested gully and terraced plantations, emerging high up with views north. Kadoorie Farm also serves as a sanctuary for injured and orphaned animals, with muntjac deer, leopard cats, birds of prey and wild boar on show – probably your one chance to see any of these shy, usually nocturnal animals at close range. There's no on-site café, but there are shelters with picnic tables, so you can bring your own food.

THE LAM TSUEN WISHING TREES

Lam Kan Rd. Bus #64K from Ⓜ Tai Po Market. MAP P.86–87

Around ten minutes southwest from Tai Po, the Lam Tsuen Wishing Trees are a pair of gnarled old figs near the

PAT SIN LENG COUNTRY PARK

roadside, propped up with poles against collapse. People used to write their wishes on paper slips, attach them to a weighted string and hurl them into the branches; but branches eventually broke off under the accumulated offerings and now wishes are pinned to a nearby notice board. Back behind here is a pretty **Tin Hau Temple** dating to 1736, and an astounding toilet block, surgically clean and full of piped music and potted orchids. The grounds are packed at Chinese New Year. Note that bus #64K continues past Kadoorie Farm to Kam Tin (see p.85).

PLOVER COVE AND PAT SIN LENG COUNTRY PARKS

Bus #75K from Ⓜ Tai Po Market. MAP P.86–87

Plover Cove Country Park occupies a rugged east-coast peninsula north of Plover Cove Reservoir, whose dam wall has turned a former marine bay into one of Hong Kong's major water sources. The access point is **Tai Mei Tuk** hamlet, comprising a clutch of food and drink stalls, the *Bradbury Jockey Club Youth Hostel* (see p.127) and a **visitors' centre** (Mon & Wed–Sun 9.30–11.30am & 1.30–4.30pm) providing hiking advice. From here you can follow a trail (or the road) for 5km to **Bride's Pool**, a pretty series of forested waterfalls, popular with picnickers.

Tai Mei Tuk is also the starting point for hikes into **Pat Sin Leng Country Park** – Pat Sin Leng means "Eight Immortals Peak" and the distinct, serrated range is visible from miles away. A 10km trail climbs steeply from behind the visitors' centre to emerge on the ridgetop, which you follow westwards as it continually climbs and descends the short, sharp peaks. About halfway along, **Wong Leng** is the 639m-high apex, and the triangulation point here has fabulous views south and east. At the far end of the trail is **Hok Tau Reservoir** and a sealed road leading to the terminus of green minibus #52B to **Fanling MTR** station. Give yourself eight hours, wear hiking shoes, and take water and a hat.

CLEARWATER BAY

Bus #91 (#91R on Sun) from Ⓜ Diamond Hill. MAP P.86–87

Clearwater Bay is a broad inlet at the New Territories' southeastern extremity. **Tai Au Mun** is the only settlement, boasting two beaches, the small #1 and the much bigger #2, the latter 5km to the south and packed at weekends.

From the bus stop at beach #2, the road and green minibus #16 continue 1500m along a windswept coastline to the members-only Clearwater Bay Golf and Country Club. Steps here descend to a venerable **Tin Hau Temple** on Joss House Bay. As one of the few Tin Hau temples in Hong Kong still facing the sea, this is a major site for annual Tin Hau festivities (see p.140), but is otherwise a quiet, simple structure with a huge terrace at the front to accommodate seasonal crowds. The entrance is guarded by two stone lions: turn the balls in their mouths three times for luck.

CLEARWATER BAY

SAI KUNG TOWN

Bus #92 from Ⓜ Diamond Hill. MAP P.86–87

Sai Kung Town is a low-key tourist retreat, and a gateway to the wilds of the Sai Kung Peninsula (below). Small fishing boats sell their catches from the seafront jetty; shoppers hang over the rail to bargain, then their choice is hit on the head and handed up in a basket on the end of a pole. Most visitors take their purchase to one of the waterfront **restaurants**, who cook it according to their instructions – you can also choose from tanks full of live seafood out front. *Kaidos* (on-demand ferries) from Sai Kung's jetty run to nearby islands and beaches; the most popular trip is the short run across to **Kiu Tsui Chau** (Sharp Island; about $25 return), whose small main beach at Hap Mun Bay, hemmed in by green headlands, is one of the prettiest in the area.

The island past Kiu Tsui Chau is the larger **Kau Sai Chau**, with a regular **ferry** (Mon–Thurs 6.40am–7pm & Fri–Sun 6.40am–9pm; every 20 min; $75 return) from its own jetty on the Sai Kung Town waterfront. The main reason to visit is to play golf at the **Jockey Club KSC Public Golf Course** (Ⓦ www.kscgolf.org.hk for fees and information), the only public course in Hong Kong.

THE SAI KUNG PENINSULA

MAP P.86–87

The Sai Kung Peninsula encompasses 75 square kilometres of rugged headlands, coves, woodland and beaches in Hong Kong's easternmost reaches. Some parts are very wild, but there are also marked paths and quiet places for picnics.

Bus #94 (daily 6.30am–9pm) runs from Sai Kung's bus terminus to the **Pak Tam Chung visitors' centre** (Mon & Wed–Sun 9.30am–4.30pm; ☏ 2792 7365), from where there's a short walking trail to **Sheung Yiu Folk Museum** (Mon & Wed–Sun 9am–4pm; free), at an abandoned traditional walled village. For a longer hike – around eight hours – follow trails via the rim of **High Island Reservoir** to Long Ke Wan, then head north over Sai Wan Hill to the bay at Tai Long Wan.

The best beaches in the area, with white sand and a peacock-blue sea, are at **Tai Long Wan** (Big Wave Bay). The one possible drawback is that it's a lengthy hike to get here, though this also means that not many people make it. Catch **minibus** #29R (Mon–Sat 9.15am, 11.30am & 3.30pm; Sun 11 services 8.30am–4.30pm; $15) to **Sai Wan Ting pavilion** from outside *McDonald's* on Chan Man Street, Sai Kung Town; a taxi costs $95. From the pavilion follow a marked track for an hour, via restaurant shacks at Sai Wan village, to **Ham Tin Wan**, a deep, open beach with another store-restaurant. Immediately north of here is the even longer **Tai Wan beach**; there will be very few people in the vicinity unless a party yacht has pulled in, or your visit coincides with one of Hong Kong's irregular **surfing competitions**.

From Ham Tin Wan, paths head inland again to **Tai Long village** and a long, hot trail back to the main road at **Pak Tam Au**. This is basically a roadside bus stop, with services #94 and #96 heading back to Sai Kung Town.

Restaurants

CHUEN KEE

51–55 Hoi Pong St, Sai Kung Town ☎ 2792 6938. Daily 7am–11pm. MAP P.86–87

The best seafood and *dim sum* in town, with seafront views. Popular, but not especially cheap at around $250 a head.

HONEYMOON DESSERT

10 Po Tung Rd (on the highway), Sai Kung Town ☎ 2792 4991. Daily 1pm–2am. MAP P.86–87

The original of a citywide chain serving desserts made from sago, mango, grass jelly, coconut milk, fruit and ice cream in every conceivable combination. Also famous for their durian concoctions, though this smelly fruit seems to overpower Western palates.

LUNG WAH

22 Wo Che St, Sha Tin ☎ 2691 1594. Daily 11.30am–10.30pm. MAP P.86–87

This ancient establishment serves great greasy pigeon – a Cantonese speciality – though it seems to have evaded hygiene regulations. Still, the run-down palatial splendour and strutting caged peacocks are worth a look, even if you choose not to dine.

TAO HEUNG

Shop A, Fuller Garden, 8 Chui Lok Street, Tai Po ☎ 2666 9923. Daily 7am–1am. MAP P.86–87

Main dishes are fairly ordinary, but a great place for *dim sum*: try the white radish cake, roast pork *cheung fan* (stuffed rice noodles) and the beef rissoles with celery.

TUNG KEE SEAFOOD

Waterfront, Sai Kung Town ☎ 2792 7453. Daily 9am–11pm. MAP P.86–87

This is a cheerful, noisy (and slightly overpriced) place, whose speciality is "bamboo fish": carp, stuffed with preserved turnip, and chargrilled outside on a hand-rotated bamboo pole, at around $150 a head.

YAT LOK

Po Wah House, Tai Ming Lane, Tai Po ☎ 2656 4732. Daily 11am–11pm. MAP P.86–87

There's a small English sign in the window of this typical roast-meat restaurant, which was featured in American chef Anthony Bourdain's TV series – but to be honest, the food here is no better or worse than in many other places in Hong Kong.

CHUEN KEE

Lantau

Twice the size of Hong Kong Island, but nowhere near as developed, Lantau has enough sights to merit a couple of full days' exploration. The site of Hong Kong's international airport, it also sports a branch of the Disneyland theme-park franchise, some excellent beaches, a tall peak to hike up and a superb cable-car ride. More traditional offerings include Po Lin Monastery, boasting an enormous seated bronze Buddha statue, old forts at Tung Chung and Fan Lau and the unusual fishing village of Tai O, which is built in part of corrugated iron – about as far from the usual hi-tech image of Hong Kong as it's possible to get. It's easy to visit as a day-trip, but there are also several places here for overnight stays (see p.127).

HONG KONG DISNEYLAND

Ⓜ Disneyland Ⓦ hongkongdisneyland.com. Daily 10am–9pm. $499, children $355.
MAP P.98–99

The world's smallest Disneyland, this theme park is worth a visit if you've time to kill between flights, but it's a bit tame compared with Disney's ten other franchises, and queues can also be a drag.

It's split into various zones, including **Main Street USA**, a recreated early twentieth-century mid-American shopping street (though the goods on sale are distinctly Chinese); **Adventureland**, home to Tarzan's treehouse (made of fake bamboo) and a jungle river cruise; **Tomorrowland**, whose excellent rides include a blacked-out rollercoaster; and **Fantasyland**, populated by a host of Disney characters, and whose best feature is the PhilharMagic 3D film show.

TUNG CHUNG AND NGONG PING 360

Ⓜ Tung Chung Ⓦ np360.com.hk. Mon–Fri 10am–6pm, Sat & Sun 9am–6.30pm. $115 one-way, $165 return, children $60/85.
MAP P.98–99

Tung Chung is a burgeoning New Town and transport hub close to Hong Kong's International Airport on Lantau's north coast. Its main attraction is the 5.7km, 25-minute-long **Ngong Ping 360 cable-car ride** up the mountainside to Po Lin Monastery and the Big Buddha. Choose a sunny day and the views are truly spectacular, stretching back off Lantau's steep hills, over the airport and out to sea; some people prefer

NGONG PING CABLE CAR

VIEW OF LANTAU PEAK FROM BIG BUDDHA

the downward ride, with the landscape feeling as if it's continually falling away. At the top, the tacky tourist village and expensive "Walking With Buddha" shows are best skipped in favour of the Po Lin monastery itself, just beyond.

LANTAU PEAK

MAP P.98–99

The 934m **Lantau Peak**, more properly known as Fung Wong Shan, is the second highest in Hong Kong, and a popular place to watch the sun rise – you can stay the night before at the *S.G. Davis Youth Hostel* (see p.127). The steep 2km trail from Po Lin to the summit takes about an hour to complete, and on a clear day views reach as far as Macau. You can pick up the Lantau Trail here and continue 5km (2hr 30min) east to the slightly lower **Tai Tung Shan**, or "Sunset Peak", from where it's a further hour to Mui Wo (see p.101).

The Lantau Trail

More than half of Lantau is designated country park, and the circular **Lantau Trail** loops for 70km around its southern half, passing ten campsites and the island's two youth hostels along the way. For detailed information on the trail's twelve stages, including campsite details, check out ⓦ afcd.gov.hk, the Country Parks Authority's website; the *Lantau Trail* leaflet (available at the ferry pier in Mui Wo); or *Hiker's Guide to Hong Kong*, available in English-language bookshops. Don't underestimate the steep, exposed trails – take a hat, sunscreen and water. The 9km section from Mui Wo to Sunset Peak (about 7hr return) gives a good taste of the whole trail: an initially wooded path which climbs to open highlands of thin pasture and stony slopes, with magnificent views down to the coast at every turn. Other good sections are the 10km easy walk (3hr) above the coast between Fan Lau and Tai O, and trails along the south coast covered on p.100.

PO LIN MONASTERY AND THE TIAN TAN BIG BUDDHA

Ngong Ping. Bus #2 from Mui Wo, #21 from Tai O or #23 from Tung Chung; or cable car from Tung Chung. Monastery: daily 8am–6pm; Buddha: 10am–5.30pm. MAP P.98-99

THE TIAN TAN BIG BUDDHA

Hidden behind an ornamental stone archway, the **Po Lin Monastery** was founded in 1906 and has grown to be the largest Chan (Zen) Buddhist temple in Hong Kong. The **front hall** sports dynamic carvings of phoenixes and coiled dragons, alongside a gilded Buddhist trinity, and opens into the main **Ten Thousand Buddhas Hall**. There's a popular **vegetarian dining hall** (11.30am–4.30pm; set meals $60–100), and much cheaper takeaway **vegetarian dim sum** sold outside, which you can eat at the adjacent tables. All this pales into insignificance beside the gigantic **Big Buddha**, at the top of a flight of steps in front of the monastery, surrounded by flying *apsaras* (Buddhist angels).

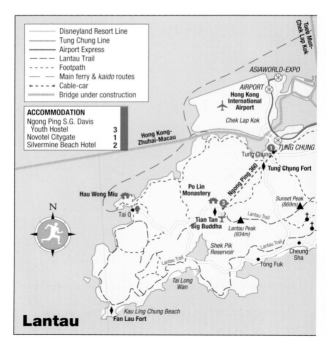

Lantau

| Disneyland Resort Line |
| Tung Chung Line |
| Airport Express |
| Lantau Trail |
| Footpath |
| Main ferry & *kaido* routes |
| Cable-car |
| Bridge under construction |

ASIAWORLD-EXPO

AIRPORT
Hong Kong International Airport

Chek Lap Kok

Tuen Mun–Chek Lap Kok

Hong Kong–Zhuhai-Macau

Tung Chung
Tung Chung Fort

Hau Wong Miu

Po Lin Monastery

Ngong Ping 360

Tai O

Tian Tan Big Buddha

Sunset Peak (869m)

Lantau Trail

Lantau Peak (934m)

Lantau Trail

Shek Pik Reservoir

Cheung Sha

Tong Fuk

Lantau Trail

Tai Long Wan

Kau Ling Chung Beach
Fan Lau Fort

N

Visiting Lantau

M ost people make a **circuit** of Lantau, catching the MTR to Tung Chung, riding the Ngong Ping 360 cable car to Po Lin, catching a bus down to Tai O and then more buses eastwards, via the south coast beaches, to Mui Wo for the ferry back to Central. **MTR** services operate approximately from 6am to 1am: from Central, it takes 35 minutes to Disneyland and forty minutes to Tung Chung. **Ferries** to Mui Wo, on the island's east coast, depart from the Outer Islands Ferry Piers in Central every thirty minutes between 6.10am and 12.30am. Roughly every third sailing is by ordinary ferry (55min; Mon–Sat $15.20, Sun $22.50), while the rest are fast ferries (40min; Mon–Sat $29.90, Sun $42.90). Buy tickets before you travel from ticket offices at the pier. For **ferry information**, contact Hong Kong and Kowloon Ferry Ltd (☏ 2815 6063, ⊛ nwff.com.hk). Once here, local **buses** connect major sites, as do the island's pale blue **taxis**.

Completed in 1993, the bronze figure seated in a ring of outsized lotus petals is 34m high and weighs 250 tonnes. Before you climb up, stand on the circular **stone platform** facing the staircase; there's an odd harmonic effect here which makes it sound as if you're inside an echoing building, not out in the open. Climb the steps for supreme views over the surrounding hills and down to the temple complex.

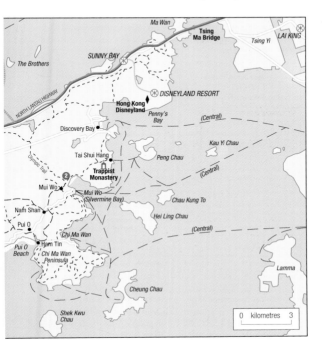

TAI O

Bus #1 from Mui Wo, #11 from Tung Chung or #21 from Po Lin Monastery. MAP P.98–99

The largest and oldest village on Lantau, Tai O is an atmospheric jumble of lanes, shrines and temples, and features a quarter full of tin-roofed stilt-houses built over the water, home to two thousand people. From the bus stop, you cross a small bridge onto the main street, which is lined by people selling dried and live seafood, including foul-smelling shrimp paste, and a refreshing red drink made from begonias. There's also a tiny **museum** (Tues–Sun 12.30–5pm; free) displaying everyday artefacts such as washboards, the prows from a Dragon Boat, a threshing machine and a cutlass. At the bridge, operators offer short **boat trips** (about $30 per person) to see the village from the water and, if you're extremely lucky, **pink dolphins**.

Cross over into the older part of the village and there are a couple of smoky temples worth a quick look. Surrounded by market stalls on the main street, **Kwan Ti Temple** dates to 1500 and honours the god of war and righteousness. **Hau Wong Miu** Temple, on Kat Hing Back Street, was built in 1699 and contains the local boat used in the annual Dragon Boat Races, some shark bones, a whale head and a carved roof-frieze displaying two roaring dragons.

THE SOUTH COAST

MAP P.98–99

Lantau's best beaches line the south coast. All of them are accessible on foot from Mui Wo along the Lantau Trail, or by bus #1 or #2 (to Tai O and Po Lin Monastery respectively

TAI O STILT-HOUSES

from Mui Wo) as far as Shek Pik Reservoir. Closest to Mui Wo is **Pui O beach** (9km; 3hr on foot), an excellent spot with barbecue pits and a free campsite. The next beach along is **Cheung Sha** (5km; 1hr 30min from Pui O on foot), Hong Kong's longest stretch of sand at 2km, partly shaded with casuarina trees and with several low-key restaurants and bars. Further west, the road strikes inland to the **Shek Pik Reservoir** (13km; 4hr on foot), landscaped to provide picnic areas and walking trails; you can also just glimpse the Big Buddha from here. From Shek Pik there's a walking track (20min) to another shady beach at **Tai Long Wan**, from where you can again pick up the Lantau Trail for 5km (1hr 30min) to **Fan Lau**, an abandoned, overgrown village at Lantau's southwestern headland. Here, the remains of a 1300-year-old rectangular fort overlook a stunning crescent bay and bright green lagoons at the back of beautiful **Kau Ling Chung** beach.

Pink dolphins

Hong Kong's waters are home to the world's entire population of **pink dolphins** (a subspecies of the Indo-Pacific humpbacked dolphin), currently estimated at sixty animals. Mostly seen off western Lantau, their rapidly declining numbers are thought to be the result of a combination of increasingly polluted waters and over-fishing. Trips to see them are run by Hong Kong Dolphinwatch (☎ 2984 1414, ⓦ hkdolphinwatch.com; 5hr; $420 for adults, $210 for children), part of the profits from which go to the WWF to support dolphin research projects. While the trips could potentially disturb the dolphins, Dolphinwatch believes that the tours form only a tiny amount of local marine traffic, and might increase awareness about these endangered animals.

MUI WO AND AROUND

MAP P.98–99

Mui Wo, also known as Silvermine Bay, is a small residential community surrounding Lantau's ferry port, with a beach, several hiking trails, some pleasant accommodation and restaurants. It's also a major bus terminus. Mui Wo marks the eastern end of the **Lantau Trail** (see box, p.97), and also the 5.7km **Olympic Trail** to Tung Chung, which passes a waterfall and old villages guarded by abandoned **watchtowers**. Also popular is the three-hour walk north over the hills, via a Trappist monastery, to Discovery Bay.

Head along the Tung Wan Tau Road to the end, cross the river bridge and follow the bay round to the right. A signpost eventually points up some steps onto the bare hills, with some excellent views along the way over to Hong Kong Island. The Trappist monastery is closed to the public, so follow the road downhill to a signposted path towards **Discovery Bay**. This New Town is a too-perfect copy of idealized middle-American suburbia, with happy blonde families zipping about in golf carts, and very few Chinese faces. There's a 24-hour **hydrofoil** from Discovery Bay back to Central ($40; 30min), plus buses to the rest of the island.

BEACH AT MUI WO

Lamma and Cheung Chau

The Hong Kong SAR encompasses some 260-odd islands, the vast majority of which are tiny, barren and uninhabited. After Lantau, Lamma and Cheung Chau are the pick of the bunch, smaller, uncluttered and relatively laidback, though hardly uncharted territory – both had been settled by the Chinese long before the British arrived.

One major draw is the beaches, at least for sunbathing – local pollution means that swimming is often not an option (signs in English give levels for the day and state whether swimming is allowed). Lamma and Cheung Chau are also noted for their seafood restaurants and food stalls, while villages offer a slice of traditional Chinese life. If nothing else, the islands make excellent escapes from city stress; accommodation is available on both of them (see p.128).

LAMMA

MAP P.103

Lamma is an elongated fourteen-square-kilometre stretch of land inhabited by five thousand people, with well-marked paths linking its settlements to small beaches, green hilltops and pleasant seascapes. **Yung Shue Wan** is a pretty, tree-shaded village at the northwestern end of the island, where the bulk of Lamma's residents live, and the main ferry terminus. There's a century-old Tin Hau temple here but nothing else to stop you beginning the walk across the island. Twenty minutes along a good concrete path is **Hung Shing Ye**, with a tiny, shaded sand beach with barbecue pits, a couple of places to eat and drink, and unfortunately close views of the power station. The path continues around the beach and up the hill on the other side, before levelling out at a viewing point marked by a Chinese pavilion. Go down the hill, past the vast cement works to your left, to some houses from where side tracks lead to **Lo So Shing**, another beach with changing rooms,

Visiting Lamma

Ferries to **Yung Shue Wan** depart from the Outer Islands Ferry Piers in Central (Mon–Sat 6.30am–12.30am, Sun 7.30am–12.30am; 30min; Mon–Sat $17.10, Sun $23.70). **Ferries to Sok Kwu Wan** also depart from the Outer Islands Ferry Piers in Central (daily 7.20am–11.30pm; 25min; Mon–Sat $21, Sun $29.80). Buy tickets before you travel from the ticket offices at the pier. For **ferry information**, contact Hong Kong and Kowloon Ferry Ltd (⌨ hkkf.com.hk).

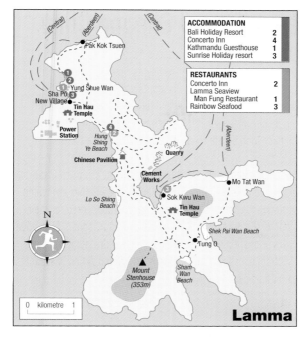

ACCOMMODATION	
Bali Holiday Resort	2
Concerto Inn	4
Kathmandu Guesthouse	1
Sunrise Holiday resort	3

RESTAURANTS	
Concerto Inn	2
Lamma Seaview	
Man Fung Restaurant	1
Rainbow Seafood	3

Lamma

showers, snack kiosk and barbecue pits.

At the end of the main path (around 5km, or 1hr 30min on foot from Yung Shue Wan), is **Sok Kwu Wan**, a fish-farming village and second ferry terminus for Hong Kong Island; floating wooden frames cover the water, interspersed with rowing boats, junks and the canvas shelters of the fishermen and women. There's another Tin Hau temple here by the main pier, along which Sok Kwu Wan's **seafood restaurants** form a line, with outdoor tables overlooking the bay and large fish tanks set back on the street. Some restaurants have English menus, but always ask the price first. Walking tracks link Sok Kwu Wan, via the small village of **Mo Tat Wan**, to spacious **Shek Pai Wan beach** on

Lamma's southeastern coast – about an hour's walk in all. There's also a trail from Sok Kwu Wan up to the summit of **Mount Stenhouse** (also known as Shan Tei Tong), 353m up in the middle of the island's southwestern bulge – it's a two-hour hike each way.

BEACH AT MO TAT WAN

CHEUNG CHAU

MAP P.104

Cheung Chau – "Long Island" – was the stronghold of the Qing Dynasty pirate Cheung Po Tsai. Along with his forty thousand followers, he terrorized shipping and villages along the adjacent Chinese coast, reputedly hiding his booty in a cave at Cheung Chau's southern end. After surrendering to government forces in 1810, he was appointed head of the local Chinese navy.

Today, Cheung Chau is the most densely populated of the outlying islands; easy walking tracks lead to the requisite beaches and seascapes, but the main attractions are watching the thriving traditional life in the main village, with its fishing boats and stalls, and – as ever – sampling the local seafood.

Ferries dock at **Cheung Chau Village**, where the island's population and activity is concentrated. The waterfront road hosts a large daily market (busy all day), where fishermen, fruit-and-veg sellers and cultivated-pearl traders rub shoulders. Just beyond the pier, down Tung Wan Road, you'll see an ancient banyan tree, whose base is often cluttered with makeshift altars.

One block in from the water on San Hing Street, the **Pak Tai Temple** (free) is dedicated to the "Northern Emperor", protector against floods. Inside is an 800-year-old iron sword believed to bring luck to fishermen, and a gilded sedan chair, for carrying the god's statue during festivals. The temple is the venue for the vibrant annual four-day **Cheung Chau Bun Festival**,

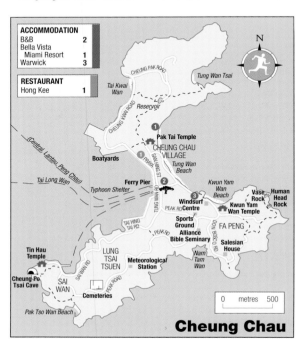

ACCOMMODATION

B&B	2
Bella Vista	
Miami Resort	1
Warwick	3

RESTAURANT

| Hong Kee | 1 |

N

CHEUNG PAK ROAD

Tung Wan Tsai

Tai Kwai Wan

CHEUNG KWAI ROAD

Reservoir

❶ Pak Tai Temple

CHEUNG CHAU VILLAGE

(Central, Lantau, Peng Chau)

Boatyards

❷

Tung Wan Beach

Tai Long Wan

Ferry Pier

Typhoon Shelter

Kwun Yam Wan Beach

Vase Rock

Human Head Rock

❸ Windsurf Centre

Kwun Yam Wan Temple

PEAK RD

Sports Ground

FA PENG

TAI HING TAI RD

PEAK RD

Alliance Bible Seminary

Salesian House

Tin Hau Temple

LUNG TSAI TSUEN

Meteorological Station

Nam Tam Wan

SAN WAN RD

SAI WAN

Cheung Po Tsai Cave

Cemeteries

PEAK ROAD

Pak Tso Wan Beach

| 0 | metres | 500 |

Cheung Chau

Visiting Cheung Chau

Ferries to Cheung Chau depart from the Outer Islands Ferry Piers in Central (daily 24hr; 40–55min; ordinary ferry Mon–Sat $13.20, Sun $19.40; fast ferry Mon–Sat $25.80, Sun $37.20).

Buy tickets before you travel from ticket offices at the pier. For **ferry information**, contact the New World First Ferry Company (www.nwff.com.hk).

held to placate the vengeful spirits of those killed by Cheung Chau's pirates (see p.140). North of the village, various paths lead up to a hilltop reservoir and views over the whole island.

From the village, crossing east over the narrow middle of the island lands you at the long **Tung Wan beach** and, around the southern headland, **Kwun Yam Wan beach**, the best on the island. Alternatively, for a two-hour walk from the village, follow the shore southwest from the ferry pier to a pavilion overlooking the harbour and a landscaped picnic area. Behind this is a side path down between the rocks on to a small rocky beach and up to a headland covered in large, rounded granite boulders, which has some superb views over the sea on a calm day.

The path continues down to **Pak Tso Wan beach** – small and sandy, though a little grubby – and then into the shady lanes on the village outskirts, which you can follow northeast to Kwun Yam Wan beach.

Restaurants

Most of the following open daily mid-morning and close by 9pm. At alfresco businesses, fix prices when ordering to avoid being ripped off.

CONCERTO INN

Hung Shing Ye beach, Lamma ☎ 2982 1668, ✆ concertoinn.com.hk. MAP P.103

Near a small and quiet beach, this hotel-restaurant is set on a delightful terrace and serves an eclectic range of Southeast Asian dishes. Mains from $180.

HONG KEE

Cheung Chau waterfront ☎ 2981 9916
MAP P.104

Inexpensive place on the waterfront serving delicious garlic-fried prawns, scallops and quick-fried fish pieces.

LAMMA SEAVIEW MAN FUNG RESTAURANT

Near the pier, Yung Shue Wan, Lamma ☎ 2982 0719. MAP P.103

Fresh crab, abalone, fish from live tanks and a long list of budget rice and noodle dishes are on the menu here, served at outdoor tables under beach umbrellas, offering pleasant views while you enjoy your meal.

RAINBOW SEAFOOD

Sok Kwu Wan, Lamma ☎ 2982 8100, ✆ rainbowrest.com.hk. MAP P.103

At this place you're invited to pick your fresh seafood directly from the tank. Along with lightly steamed whole fish, there's masterful deep-fried squid with chillies and salt. Slightly overpriced for what you get, but not expensive.

Macau

Sixty kilometres west from Hong Kong across the Pearl River delta, the former Portuguese enclave of Macau occupies a 26-square-kilometre peninsula and two artificially fused islands jutting off the Chinese mainland. With heaps of well-preserved colonial architecture and Portuguese-influenced cuisine, Macau's European heritage is more obvious than Hong Kong's, though here too the majority of the population is Cantonese-speaking. Millions of tourists flock here each year, primarily to gamble at Macau's many casinos – it's the only place in China where they have been legalized.

Macau's downtown area comprises a packed old quarter of forts, temples, churches and narrow streets, alongside a modern casino strip built on reclaimed land. South from the peninsula across three long, ribbon-like bridges, Taipa and Coloane are conjoined islands with more outrageous casinos and a spacious black-sand beach.

LARGO DO SENADO

MAP P.108–109, POCKET MAP E11

Largo do Senado (Senate Square) is Macau's public focus, cobbled and surrounded by elegant colonial buildings painted pale pink, yellow or white, with shuttered upper storeys and street-level colonnades. There's a small fountain in the middle, while west down Rua de São Domingos and adjacent streets

Money in Macau

Macau's currency is the pataca (MOP$), divided into avos. Coins come in 10, 20 and 50 avo denominations, notes in 10, 50, 100 and MOP$1000. The Hong Kong dollar and pataca are almost equal in value; you can use Hong Kong dollars in Macau but not pataca in Hong Kong.

is a food and clothing market. On the east side of the square, **Santa Casa de Misericórdia** (Tues–Sun 10am–12.30pm & 2.30–5.30pm; MOP$5) is Macau's oldest social institution, founded in 1569 by Dom Belchior Carneiro, the city's first Catholic bishop. His skull is displayed in a wood-panelled museum upstairs, along with porcelain marked with the Jesuit logo "JHS".

The Senate House itself, the **Leal Senado** (daily 9am–9pm; free), faces Largo do Senado on Avenida de Almeida Ribeiro. It's of traditional Portuguese design, with interior courtyard walls decorated with classic blue-and-white *azulejo* tiling, and an ornamental courtyard out the back. The upstairs library (Mon–Fri 1–7pm) is stacked with a large collection of books about China (many in English), dating from the

sixteenth century onwards. On the next level up, the Senate Chamber – a grand room with panelled walls and ceiling and excellent views over the square – is open to the public when not being used for official functions.

East off Largo do Senado, two small lanes slope a short way uphill to another, smaller cobbled square and the squat and undistinguished **Sé** (daily 7.30am–6.30pm; free), Macau's cathedral, last rebuilt in 1937 and featuring some fine stained glass. At the north end of Largo do Senado, the arcaded buildings peter out in the adjacent Largo São Domingos, which holds Macau's most beautiful church, the seventeenth-century Baroque **São Domingos** (daily 10am–6pm; free). Its cream-and-stucco facade is echoed inside by the pastel-coloured pillars and walls, and by a quiet statue of the Virgin and Child. On May 13 every year the church is the starting point for a major procession in honour of Our Lady of Fatima.

SÃO PAULO

MAP P.108–109, POCKET MAP E11

North of São Domingos, through a nest of cobbled lanes flanked by *pastelarias* (shops selling sweets, biscuits and roast meats), stands the imposing facade of **São Paulo** church. Founded in 1602, its rich design reflected the cosmopolitan nature of early Macau – designed by an Italian in a Spanish style, and built by Japanese craftsmen. São Paulo became a noted centre of learning until the expulsion of the Jesuits from Macau, after which it became an army barracks. In 1835 a fire, which started in the kitchens, destroyed the entire complex except for the carved stone front. On approaching up the wide swathe of steps it seems at first that the church still stands, but on reaching the terrace the facade alone is revealed, like a theatre backdrop, rising in four chipped and cracked tiers. The symbolic statues and reliefs include a dove at the top (the Holy Spirit) flanked by the sun and moon; below is Jesus, around whom reliefs show the implements of the Crucifixion – a ladder, manacles, a crown of thorns and a flail. Below are the Virgin Mary and angels, flowers representing China (a peony) and Japan (chrysan-themum), a griffin and a rigged galleon, while the bottom tier holds four Jesuit saints, and the crowning words "Mater Dei" above the central door.

FORTALEZA DO MONTE

Daily 7am–7pm. Free. MAP P.108–109, POCKET
MAP E11

East of São Paulo the solid
Fortaleza do Monte, once part
of the São Paulo complex, saw
action only once, when its
cannons helped repel the
Dutch in 1622. The ramparts,
lined with the weathered
cannons, give views over
almost the whole peninsula.

The fort houses the **Museu de
Macau** (Tues–Sun 10am–6pm;
MOP$15). The first floor charts
the arrival of the Portuguese
and the heyday of the trading
routes, with displays of bartered
goods – wooden casks,
porcelain, spices, silver and silk.
The second floor has more of a
Chinese theme, with full-sized
street reconstructions as well as
footage of customs and festivals.
Offbeat items include a display

on cricket-fighting (where two
of these aggressive insects are
pitted against each other),
complete with a tiny coffin and
headstone for expired fighters.

HONG KUNG TEMPLE

Rua Cinco de Outubro. MAP P.108–109

The unpretentious **Hong Kung
Temple** is dedicated to Kwan
Tai, god of riches and war, and
is the focus for the extraordinary **Drunken Dragon
Festival**, held on the eighth day
of the fourth lunar month
(April or May). Organized by
the Fish Retailers' Association,
the festival features opera,
religious ceremonies, martial
arts performances and a parade
from here to the Porto Interior
(Inner Harbour) via all the
local fish shops, by men
carrying large wooden dragon
heads and consuming vast
quantities of spirits.

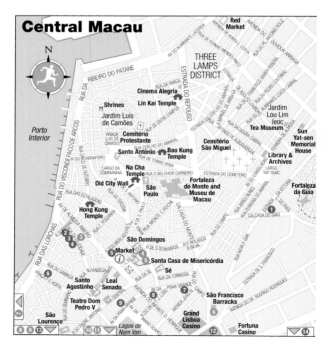

Central Macau

Visiting Macau from Hong Kong

By sea

Ferries to Macau's Porto Exterior (Outer Harbour) Jetfoil Terminal leave from the Macau Ferry Terminal, Shun Tak Centre, Central, Hong Kong Island (daily 24hr; 1–4 hourly; ⓦ turbojet.com.hk), and the China Ferry Terminal, Canton Road, Tsim Sha Tsui, Kowloon (daily 7am–10.30pm; 2 hourly; ⓦ turbojet. com.hk). Both services take 55 minutes and cost about HK$160 one-way (HK$320 return), though prices rise daily after 6pm, and all day on weekends. It's advisable to book in advance (through the website or at the terminals) at weekends and on public holidays; buying a return ticket saves time at the other end. Aim to be at the ferry terminal at least thirty minutes before departure to clear customs. You'll be allowed on with a suitcase or rucksack, but if you have anything more you'll have to check it in and pay an extra $20–40.

By air

A helicopter service to Macau's Jetfoil Terminal operates from the Macau Ferry Terminal on Hong Kong Island (daily 9am–11pm; 2 hourly; ⓦ skyshuttlehk.com). The journey takes fifteen minutes and costs HK$4300 one-way. In Hong Kong, buy tickets from the window adjacent to the ferry ticket office in the Shun Tak Centre; in Macau, tickets are sold from marked booths on the second floor of the Jetfoil Terminal.

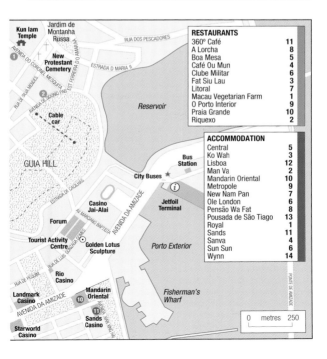

RESTAURANTS	
360° Café	11
A Lorcha	8
Boa Mesa	5
Café Ou Mun	4
Clube Militar	6
Fat Siu Lau	3
Litoral	7
Macau Vegetarian Farm	1
O Porto Interior	9
Praia Grande	10
Riquexo	2

ACCOMMODATION	
Central	5
Ko Wah	3
Lisboa	12
Man Va	2
Mandarin Oriental	10
Metropole	9
New Nam Pan	7
Ole London	6
Pensão Wa Fat	8
Pousada de São Tiago	13
Royal	1
Sands	11
Sanva	4
Sun Sun	6
Wynn	14

JARDIM LUÍS DE CAMÕES

Praça Luís de Camões. Daily 6am–10pm.
Free. MAP P.108–109, POCKET MAP E11

The Jardim Luís de Camões
(Camões Garden) is a very
tropical, laidback spread of
banyans, ferns, fan palms,
paved terraces and flowers. It's
always full of people pottering
about, exercising or playing
cards under the trees, and
commemorates the sixteenth-
century Portuguese poet who is
supposed to have visited Macau
and written part of his epic
Os Lusíadas (about Vasco da
Gama's voyages) here. There's a
bust of Camões, encircled by
granite boulders, although
there's no concrete evidence
that he ever came here.

CEMITÉRIO PROTESTANTE

Rua de Entre Campos. Daily 8.30am–5.30pm.
Free. MAP P.108–109

The Cemitério Protestante (Old
Protestant Cemetery) houses
many of the non-Portuguese
traders and visitors who expired
in the enclave. For decades,
Protestants had no set burial
place in Macau: the Catholic
Portuguese didn't want them
and the Chinese objected if they
were interred on ancestral lands.
Some of the graves were moved
here from various resting places
outside the city walls, as the
pre-1814 headstones show, and
now sit slightly forlornly and
somewhat overgrown in this
sprawling plot.

The most famous resident is
the artist **George Chinnery**,
who died here in 1852 having
spent his life in India and the
Far East recording the
development of European trade
in the region. Some of the
cemetery's most poignant graves
are those belonging to ordinary
seamen: Samuel Smith "died by
a fall from aloft"; a cabin boy
similarly met his end "through

the effects of a fall into the
hold"; while Oliver Mitchell
"died of dysentery". The grave
of the missionary Robert
Morrison, who translated the
Bible into Chinese, is also here,
as is that of his wife, who died
in childbirth.

JARDIM LOU LIM IEOC

Av. do Conselheiro Ferreira de Almeida. Daily
6am–9pm. Free. MAP P.108–109.
POCKET MAP F11

A high wall encloses the
beautiful Jardim Lou Lim Ieoc,
a formal arrangement of
pavilions, carp ponds, bamboo
groves and frangipani trees.
Built in the nineteenth century
by the wealthy Chinese
merchant Lou Kou, it was
modelled on the famous
classical Chinese gardens of
Suzhou, and typically manages
to appear much more spacious
than it really is. Jardim Lou
Lim Ieoc and Hong Kong's Nan
Lian Gardens (see p.81) are the
only such examples in Hong
Kong and Macau. The galleries
lining the east side host
occasional amateur opera
performances on Sundays, and
a **tea museum** (free), though
captions are in Chinese only.

WALKWAY AT JARDIM LOU LIM IEOC

GUIA HILL

Av. Sidónio Pais. MAP P.108-109

Guia Hill, Macau's apex and site of its former defence headquarters, is now a landscaped park. Paths wind to the top from the entrances on Estrada da Vittoria and Avenida Sidónio Pais; from the latter, there's also a cable-car link to the top (Tues–Sun 8am–6pm; MOP$2 one-way, MOP$3 return). Either way, you'll end up a short walk from the remains of **Fortaleza da Guia** (daily 9am–6pm; free), a fortress completed in 1638, originally designed to defend the border with China, though it's seen most service as an observation post due to its high position. There is a network of short, disconnected tunnels used in the 1930s to store munitions, and a small seventeenth-century chapel within the walls dedicated to Our Lady of Guia. This contains an image of the Virgin – whom local legend says left the chapel and deflected enemy bullets with her robe during the Dutch attack of 1622 – and original blue and pink frescoes, which combine Chinese elements with Christian religious images. The chapel's other function was to ring its bell to warn of storms, something now taken care of by the fortress's lighthouse, built in 1865. The best views from the fortress walls are southeast down over the modern Porto Exterior, and westwards towards Fortaleza do Monte and the old town.

KUN IAM TEMPLE

Av. do Coronel Mesquita. Daily 7am–5.30pm. Free. MAP P.108-109, POCKET MAP F11

Entered through a banyan-planted courtyard crowded with fortune-tellers, the scruffy, 400-year-old Kun Iam Temple is dedicated to the Bodhisattva of mercy (known in Hong Kong as Kwun Yam), and was the venue for the signing of the first ever **Sino-American treaty** on July 3, 1844 by Viceroy Tai Yeng and the US Commissioner Caleb Cushing. The buildings are of the usual heavy stone, but their roofs are decked in colourful porcelain statuettes depicting folk tales and historical scenes. Inside the third hall are statues of Kun Iam and eighteen other **Bodhisattvas**, those who had attained the right to enter paradise but chose to stay on earth to help humanity.

LIN KAI TEMPLE AND AROUND

Travessa da Corda. MAP P.108–109

Tucked down a side lane off main Estrada do Repouso, **Lin Kai Temple** (daily 7.30am– 5.15pm; free) is a maze of small halls dedicated to a host of local deities, including the Fire God, Ua Kwong, whose festival is held on the 28th day of the ninth lunar month (some point in Oct). The temple is old, shabby and in need of attention, but it oozes character and there's a small bric-a-brac **night market** outside at the weekends. Just a few doors up on Estrada do Repouso, the little green and white **Cinema Alegria** still has its original 1950s Art Deco fittings, making it an atmospheric place to catch the latest Hollywood or Chinese blockbuster in Cantonese.

THREE LAMPS DISTRICT AND THE RED MARKET

Rotunda de Carlos da Maia. MAP P.108–109, POCKET MAP F11

A few minutes' walk from the Lin Kai Temple, a roundabout marks the centre of the pedestrianized Sam Jan Dang or **Three Lamps District**. The streets immediately north of here are packed with busy market stalls selling bedding, fabrics, fresh produce and – especially – **clothes**; bargain hard and don't believe any marked sizes. Hidden away here is the bizarre **Cheoc Lam Temple**, walled with green tiles, planted with bamboo and again divided into a host of ancestral halls and shrines to an impartial mix of Buddhist and Taoist saints.

There's more activity just north again inside the **Red Market**, another Art Deco building at the intersection of Avenida de Horta e Costa and Avenida do Almirante Lacerda. Designed in 1936 by local architect Jio Alberto Basto, it houses a produce market full of slabs of meat and frozen seafood along with live chickens, pigeons, ducks, fish, frogs and turtles, all waiting to be carted off for dinner.

THE LIN FONG TEMPLE AND MUSEU LIN ZEXU

Av. do Almirante Lacerda. POCKET MAP F10

About 500m north of the Red Market, the **Lin Fong Temple** (daily 7am–5pm; free) was established in 1592 to provide accommodation for travelling officials. It's full of gaudy woodwork painted gold and red, coloured wall mouldings of fantastic beasts and very fine stone carvings above the entrances depicting moral operatic scenes. The temple is dedicated to **Kwan Tai**, a loyal general during the turbulent Three Kingdoms period (around 184–280 AD), who chose to be executed rather than betray his oath brothers. A statue of a horse in the right-hand entrance is a memorial to Kwan Tai's lightning-fast steed **Red Hare**, who pined away and died after his master's execution – people often place vegetables in the statue's mouth.

Off the temple's forecourt, **Museu Lin Zexu** (Tues–Sun 9am–5pm; MOP$5) commemorates another upstanding official, Lin Zexu (or Lam Kung), who tried to stamp out the nineteenth-century opium trade by destroying British supplies of the drug, only to be blamed for precipitating the first Opium War and exiled to China's northwest. The museum displays a staid collection of period artefacts, though the account books for 1830–1839 show that the opium trade cost the Chinese treasury between seven and eight million silver pieces annually, amply illustrating why the Chinese court was keen to stop it – and why British traders and local Chinese merchants wanted to keep it going.

THE BORDER

POCKET MAP F10

Bus #5 from the Lin Fong Temple runs a kilometre north to the **border with China**, past an escalation of shops and backstreet markets selling all the things you might have forgotten to buy – or never even realized were for sale – during your stay. There's also a lot of contraband on show, having slipped over from the cheaper side of the border. The only historical monument of any sort is the old stone archway of the **Portas do Cerco** ("Siege Gate", though referred to in English as the Barrier Gate), which has stood in this spot, more or less, since 1849, though now made redundant by the huge modern border terminal behind. There's not really any reason to be here unless you're crossing into China at Zhuhai, in which case – assuming you already have your visa – just follow the crowds into the terminal. If you're just arriving, join the similar hordes streaming south to waiting taxis and casino buses (the public bus station is underground).

FISH STALL AT THE RED MARKET

RUA DA FELICIDADE

RUA DA FELICIDADE

MAP P.108-109

On the west side of the southern peninsula is the **Porto Interior** or Inner Harbour, formerly Macau's main port area. Between here and the Leal Senado (see p.106) is a warren of backstreets. The most interesting is **Rua da Felicidade** (Happiness Street). This was once a sordid red-light district but now – even though prostitutes linger – it comprises an atmospheric run of guesthouses, *pastelarias* selling biscuits and cured pork, and restaurants; the shop fronts have all been whitewashed, and their shutters and big wooden doors restored and painted red.

THE BARRA

MAP P.108-109, POCKET MAP E12-E13

The Barra is the district at the southern end of Macau's peninsula, cut by Rua Central and its continuations, a dense collection of nineteenth-century civic buildings and cheap Chinese cafés, clothes-making workshops and small businesses. On Rua Central, the peppermint-coloured **Teatro Dom Pedro V** (Mon & Wed–Sun 10am–6pm; free) dates to 1873; opposite is the contemporary church of **Santo Agostinho**. Further south, the

square-towered **São Lourenço** church is framed by palms and fig trees, its interior decorated in wooden panels depicting the Stations of the Cross. Above, on Penha Hill, a stiff walk is rewarded by the nineteenth-century **Bishop's Palace and Penha Chapel** (daily 10am–5.30pm; free); the exteriors are drab, but views south of the bridges snaking over to Taipa compensate.

Back down below, **Rua do Padre Antonio** crosses tiny **Largo do Lilau**, a residential square where a spring seeps out of a wall-fountain. This was one of the first areas of Macau to be settled, and older buildings include a **Mandarin's House** from 1881 on Travessa Antonio da Silva (Mon, Tues & Thurs–

COLONIAL BUILDING IN THE BARRA

Sun 10am–6pm; free), a whitewashed complex of halls and courtyards. From here the main road becomes **Calçada da Barra**, and 500m south brings you to the yellow and white arched colonnade surrounding the **Quartel dos Mouros** (Moorish Barracks), built in 1874 to house a Goan regiment and now home to the Port Office. The lobby has an unlikely collection of naval cannon and ceremonial pikestaffs. From here, it's a couple of minutes downhill to the A-Ma Temple.

THE A-MA TEMPLE

Rua do Almirante Sérgio. Daily 7am–6pm. Free. POCKET MAP E12

The A-Ma Temple is Macau's oldest place of worship, founded in 1370 and named after a girl whose spirit would appear to save people at sea (known in Hong Kong as Tin Hau and elsewhere in Southeast Asia as Mazu). When the Portuguese made their first landfall here in the early 1550s, they unintentionally named the whole territory after her ("Macau" being a corruption of *a ma kok*, the name of the headland).

The complex comprises a series of small stone halls and pavilions jumbled together on the hillside among granite boulders, all cluttered with incense spirals and red-draped wooden models of boats and statues of the goddess. Many of the rocks are also carved with symbols of the A-Ma story and poems in Chinese, describing Macau and its religious associations. There is also an array of fish tanks full of turtles, onto whose shells people aim to drop coins for good luck. The busiest time to visit is for the **A-Ma Festival** (the 23rd day of the third moon, April or May; see p.140).

MUSEU MARÍTIMO

Rua do Almirante Sérgio. Mon & Wed–Sun 10am–6pm. MOP$10. POCKET MAP E12

Macau's Museu Marítimo (Maritime Museum) is an engaging and well-presented collection relating to local fishing techniques and festivals, Chinese and Portuguese maritime prowess, and boat-building. There's navigational equipment, a scale model of seventeenth-century Macau, traditional clothing used by the fishermen, a host of lovingly made models of Chinese and Portuguese vessels, and even a small collection of boats moored at the pier. These include a wooden *lorcha* – used for chasing pirate ships – and racing craft used during the **Dragon Boat Festival** (see p.141). The whole collection is made eminently accessible with the help of explanatory English-language notes and video displays.

Land reclamation

Land reclamation has seen the Macau peninsula grow three times bigger over the last 150 years. Part of an accompanying drive for modernization, the biggest development projects so far include the expansion of the Porto Exterior area, the southern peninsula's waterfront being closed up to form two artificial lakes, and the fusing together of the former islands of Taipa and Coloane. A positive aspect of this land reclamation is that the older parts of town haven't been targeted for wholesale demolition – something all too common on the Chinese mainland.

Long abandoned, the fortress ruins were restored in 1976 and now form the basis of the *Pousada de São Tiago* hotel (see p.129), one of the most romantic places to stay in all Macau. Only the entranceway, foundations and eighteenth-century chapel survive from its original form, but – assuming you aren't too sloppily dressed – nobody will mind you entering the hotel to have a quick look at them.

AVENIDA DA AMIZADE AND THE PORTO EXTERIOR

MAP P.108–109, POCKET MAP F12–G12

The modern area southeast of Guia Hill is built on land reclaimed from the Porto Exterior (Outer Harbour) over the last few decades. The main artery here is the multi-laned **Avenida da Amizade**, whose southern end is marked by the orange-tiled **Lisboa**. It's Macau's most famous hotel and a roaring, 1930s-style casino, crowned by a multistorey circular drum done up like a wedding cake – though now completely outclassed by the adjacent, multicoloured **Grand**

FORTALEZA DE SÃO TIAGO DA BARRA

Pousada de São Tiago, Rua São Tiago da Barra. POCKET MAP E13

Set at Macau's southernmost tip, the **Fortaleza da Barra** was once Macau's most important fortress. Completed in 1629, it was designed with 10m-high walls and lined with cannons to protect the entrance to the Inner Harbour, then just offshore (though land reclamation has converted it into the Lago Sai Vai lake).

Casinos

Macau's 34 **casinos** are frenetic and packed places, generally with little padding to their primary function as gambling halls – though a few, like the Grand Lisboa or the Venetian in Cotai, are absurdly ostentatious.

Games on offer include one-armed bandits or slot machines (called "hungry tigers" locally), card games like baccarat and blackjack, and some peculiarly Chinese options: *boule* is like roulette but with a larger ball and fewer numbers; *pai kao* is Chinese dominoes; *fan tan* involves a cup being scooped through a pile of buttons which are then counted out in groups of four, bets being laid on how many are left at the end of the count; and *dai-siu* ("big-small") bets on the value of three dice either having a small (3–9) or big (10–18) value.

Entry is conditional on your being over 18 years old, not wearing shorts, sandals or slippers, handing over bags and cameras at the door and carrying a valid passport. Minimum bets are usually MOP$100.

Lisboa, owned by the same management. Nearby on Avenida da Praia Grande, the **São Francisco barracks**, built in 1864 and painted a deep pink (as are all of Macau's military buildings), is the area's sole antique.

The whole Avenida da Amizade area is awash with casinos, and a **casino crawl** will provide a wide scope for people-watching, even if you're not interested in gambling. The **Casino Jai Alai** on Avenida do Dr Rodrigo Rodrigues is dark and verging on sleazy, with the feel of a hardcore den; the gold-windowed **Sands** on Avenida da Amizade has a Las Vegas slickness and colossal open interior; the **Wynn** offers a sophisticated atmosphere; while the **Starworld** – despite a smart exterior and bright lighting – is another low-end deal specializing in tacky carpets and an ocean of slot machines.

Macau Cultural Centre houses the five-storey **Museum of Art** (Tues–Sun 10am–7pm; MOP$5), whose collection of period paintings of Macau shares space with travelling exhibitions and temporary shows from overseas. The adjacent waterfront is dominated by a 20m bronze sculpture of Kun Iam.

Across Avenida da Amizade from the Sands casino, holidaying mainlanders pose in front of a **Golden Lotus Flower** sculpture, which sits beside the **Tourist Activity Centre**. The Centre's best feature is the **Museu do Vinho** (Wine Museum; 10am–8pm, closed Tues; free), dedicated to the history of Portuguese viniculture; entry gets you a free sample, and the shop sells some interesting vintages. Back over Avenida da Amizade between the Sands and the Jetfoil Terminal, **Fisherman's Wharf** is a themed open-air shopping plaza and entertainment complex incorporating a Chinese fort, a 40m-high man-made volcano, a Roman amphitheatre, re-creations of Chinese and European streets, and the usual restaurants and nightclubs. It's all rather lacklustre, with the air of a half-completed project that nobody really knows what to do with, though things perk up for specific events like the Grand Prix or Chinese New Year. From here, it's just a short walk on to the **Jetfoil Terminal**, outside of which you'll find a bus terminal (buses #3, #3A and #10A go to the *Lisboa* hotel or Largo do Senado).

Visiting Taipa and Coloane

For **Taipa Village**, take bus #11 from Avenida Almeida Ribeiro near Largo do Senado, bus #28A from the Jetfoil Terminal, or buses #22 or #33 from the *Lisboa* hotel; all these drop off near Taipa Stadium, a short walk from the village.

For **Coloane**, catch bus #21 or #21A from the *Lisboa* hotel; cutting straight across Taipa, these both travel down Coloane's west side to Coloane Village, from where the #21A and #26 continue via Cheoc Van beach to Hác Sá beach. From Taipa Village, take bus #15, which runs around Coloane's east side via the *Westin Resort* and Hác Sá beach, before terminating at Coloane Village.

TAIPA VILLAGE

POCKET MAP F12

Taipa's main point of interest is old Taipa Village, a few narrow streets surrounding a couple of faded old squares. The Portuguese and Macanese **restaurants** here are one attraction, and on Sundays (noon–9pm) the streets are packed with a handicraft market. **Rua do Cunha** is the main street, a narrow pedestrianized lane lined with restaurants, *pastelarias* and shops selling daily necessities. This exits into little **Feira da Carmo** square, surrounded by old pastel-coloured homes, at whose centre is the colonnaded nineteenth-century market-place. Two nearby **temples** to

Tin Hau and Pak Tai are similarly low-key, though Pak Tai's sports an impressive stone frieze above the entrance.

Exit Feira da Carmo square onto Rua Correia da Silva, and you'll soon see a flowing set of stairs lined with fig trees, which ascend to the small **Igreja do Carmo** (Lady of Carmel Church; Mon & Wed–Sun 8am–5pm; free). Just below sit five early twentieth-century mansions set up as **Casa Museu** (House Museum; Tues–Sun 10am–6pm; MOP$5, free Sun). The first is comfortably airy and filled with tasteful period wooden furniture; others display old photos of Taipa and Coloane, costumed mannequins and temporary art shows.

THE VENETIAN CASINO, COTAI

COTAI AND THE VENETIAN

POCKET MAP G13

The recently created land connecting Taipa with Coloane is known as **Cotai**, an up-and-coming entertainment district featuring the extraordinary **Venetian**, a full-scale reproduction of Venice's St Mark's Square. This houses the world's largest casino resort, with 850 gaming tables, 4100 slot machines and its own permanent **Cirque de Soleil** troupe, the first of many similar planned projects set to be developed in the near future. Further reclamation means that Cotai's western side now bumps up against the Chinese mainland, with the **Cotai Frontier Post** (not yet open to pedestrians) making access easy for coachloads of holidaying mainlanders.

COLOANE

POCKET MAP F13–G13

Coloane was once a base for pirates who hid out in its cliffs and caves, seizing the cargoes of trading ships passing between Macau and China. The island's main draws are its peaceful surroundings, beaches and a village with the usual mix of temples and colonial leftovers.

Parque de Seac Pai Van (daily 8am–6pm; free) is a landscaped hillside with gardens, ponds, pavilions and paths up to a 20m-high white-marble statue of A-Ma which looks out over the water. **Coloane Village**, a cluster of cobbled lanes around a little central square and a seafront row of crumbling Chinese houses, shrines and temples, is also home to the pale yellow **St Francis Xavier chapel** (dawn to dusk; free), named after the sixteenth-century missionary who passed through Macau on his way to China and Japan. Out front is a monument with embedded cannons commemorating the repelling of the last pirate attack in 1910. Further along the waterfront, the **Tam Kung Temple** (daily 8.30am–5.30pm; free) houses a whalebone shaped into a Dragon Boat with oarsmen.

Coloane's southern coast has some good **beaches**, though the polluted water is unfit for swimming. **Cheoc Van** is well developed, featuring cafés and a swimming pool (Mon–Sat 8am–9pm, Sun 8am–midnight; MOP$10). **Hác Sá** is better, a long stretch of grey-black sand backed by pine trees, with plenty of picnic places, a beach bar and a recreation complex with another pool (Mon–Sat 8am–9pm, Sun 8am–midnight; MOP$15).

Macanese food

Macanese food – Macau's indigenous cuisine – blends Cantonese, Portuguese and colonial influences in varying degrees. Some dishes are straight Portuguese, such as *caldo verde* (cabbage and potato soup), *bacalhau* (dried salted cod) or plain grilled sardines; colonial dishes include "African Chicken" (served in a peppery peanut sauce) and Brazilian *feijoada* stew; while many cooks cross-fertilize foreign influences with Cantonese ingredients, creating "Chinese" dishes which are unlike anything found elsewhere. On top of this, there's a liking for un-Chinese accompaniments such as freshly baked bread, strong coffee and wine and port, plus **desserts** – including *nata*, the ubiquitous baked custard tartlets.

Restaurants

360º CAFÉ

Level 60, Macau Tower ☎ 9888 8622. Daily
11.30am–3pm & 7–10.30pm. MAP P.108–109
Smart revolving restaurant with
unparalleled city views, serving
Indian, Macanese and plain
grilled seafood. One way not to
bankrupt yourself is to opt for
the set buffets (from MOP$278).

A LORCHA

Rua do Almirante Sérgio 289 ☎ 2831 3193.
Wed–Sun 12.30–3.30pm & 7–11.30pm.
MAP P.108–109, POCKET MAP E12
This wood-beamed restaurant
serves outstanding Portuguese
food, and is consequently
always busy. There's a large
menu of staples, including
serradura, a spectacular cream
and biscuit dessert. Pricey.

A PETISQUEIRA

Rua de S. João, Taipa Village 15 ☎ 2882 5354.
Tues–Fri 12.30–2.15pm & 6.45–10pm, Sat & Sun
12.30–2.30pm and 6.45–10pm. POCKET MAP F13
With its relaxing green interior,
this friendly, well-regarded
Portuguese restaurant has all
the usual favourites including
whole grilled sea bass.

BOA MESA

Travessa do S. Domingos 16A, between the
Sé and Largo do Senado ☎ 2838 9453. Daily
noon–10pm. MAP P.108–109
A relaxed, friendly place taking
pride in its farm-bred pig
dishes and sumptuous
chocolate mousse. Set meals are
moderately priced, and even
a la carte it's not too expensive.

CAFÉ NGA TIM/CHAN CHI MEI

Largo Eduardo Marques, in front of the
Xavier Chapel, Coloane Village ☎ 2888 2086.
Daily noon–1am. POCKET MAP F13
Inexpensive menu of Chinese,
Macanese and Portuguese
dishes, excelling in fresh seafood.
Around MOP$100 a head.

SEAFOOD DISH AT A LORCHA

CAFÉ OU MUN

Travessa de São Domingos 12 ☎ 2837 2207.
Mon 11am–7pm, Tues–Sun 9am–10pm. MAP
P.108–109
Café-restaurant with excellent
coffee, croissants and toasted
sandwiches; also serves light
meals at lunchtime.

CLUBE MILITAR

Av. da Praia Grande 975 ☎ 2871 4000. Daily
noon–3pm & 7–11pm. "No sportswear" dress
code. MAP P.108–109
This private club in the São
Francisco barracks has an elegant
colonial dining room open to the
public. The a la carte Portuguese
menu is dear, but the set-price
lunch buffet is fantastic value
(around MOP$150 a head).

FAT SIU LAU

Rua da Felicidade 64 ☎ 9857 3580. Daily
noon–11pm. MAP P.108–109
One of Macau's oldest and
most famous Chinese
restaurants, with a relaxed
atmosphere. Pigeon is the
house speciality, but otherwise
the food is not outstanding.

FERNANDO

Hác Sá Beach, Coloane ☎ 2888 2531. Daily
noon–9.30pm; closed May 1. MAP P.108–109.
The good Portuguese food

and a casual, beach-side atmosphere make this long-running place a favourite with expats. Book in advance and be prepared to catch a taxi home. About MOP$200 per head.

GALO

Rua do Cunha 45, Taipa Village ☎ 2882 7423. Mon–Fri 10.30am–3.30pm & 5.30–10.30pm, Sat & Sun 10.30am–10.30pm. POCKET MAP F13

Decorated in Portuguese country style, with a menu sporting boiled meats, steaks, grilled squid or crab, and large mixed salads. Not fine cuisine, but hearty and full of flavour.

LITORAL

Rua do Almirante Sérgio 261 ☎ 2896 7878. Daily noon–3pm and 5.30–10.30pm. MAP P.108–109, POCKET MAP E12

Rated by some as serving the best Portuguese and Macanese food in Macau, with a menu based on old family recipes including curried crab and stewed pork with shrimp paste. Bookings essential.

LORD STOW'S BAKERY

Coloane Village Square, Coloane. Daily 7am–10pm. POCKET MAP F13

Although British-owned, this is one of the best places to eat *natas* (small custard tarts), made from a secret improved recipe without animal fat. Buy takeaways from the bakery, or have coffee and a light meal at their café around the corner.

MACAU VEGETARIAN FARM

Av. do Coronel Mesquita 11 ☎ 2875 2824. Daily 11am–3pm & 5.30–10pm. MAP P.108–109

A huge place opposite the Kun Iam Temple, serving strictly vegetarian Chinese food, with tofu, gluten and mushrooms prepared to resemble meat.

O PORTO INTERIOR

Rua do Almirante Sérgio 259 ☎ 2896 7770. Daily 11.30am–10pm. MAP P.108–109. POCKET MAP E12

A smart, relaxed place excelling in mid-range Portuguese and Macanese fare, served amid a mix of Chinese wooden screens and terracotta tiling.

O SANTOS

Rua da Cunha, Taipa Village ☎ 2822 7508. Wed–Sun noon–3pm & 6.30–10.30pm. MAP P.108–109

Hearty, home-style Portuguese food, delivered with little ceremony but in healthy portions: seafood, pork and bean stew, rabbit and roast suckling pig. Mains from MOP$90.

RIQUEXO

Av. de Sidónio Pais 69-B ☎ 2856 5655. Mon–Fri 11am–6pm. MAP P.108–109

Basic Portuguese canteen, with little atmosphere and a limited menu but popular for its low prices. Go for the *feijoada* or curry chicken at MOP$28–55.

LORD STOW'S BAKERY

ACCOMMODATION

Accommodation

Hong Kong has abundant accommodation, but space comes at a premium. The cheapest options downtown are at guesthouses in Tsim Sha Tsui and Mong Kok, offering beds in dormitories with shared bathrooms (around HK$150 per person), and doubles with en suites (around HK$450 per room). Hotels start at HK$1000 for a small room in the Kowloon backstreets, through to HK$2500 for a mid-range boutique place in a better location, and rise to over twice this for harbour views in Central or Tsim Sha Tsui. Options in the New Territories and islands include guesthouses, mid-range hotels and seven remote, self-catering youth hostels (w yha.org.hk; beds from HK$115). Prices are highest during big sports events, Christmas and summer.

Macau has budget options with doubles for under MOP$500, mid-range hotels for MOP$1200 and a luxury end catered to by casino resorts (over MOP$2000). Rates are higher on Friday and Saturday nights, and during the November Grand Prix.

Prices given are for the cheapest double room unless specified; hostel prices are for a dorm bed per person. Hostel and guesthouse prices are inclusive; in hotels, a ten percent service fee – and in Macau a further five percent tax – is charged on top.

Central

GARDEN VIEW (YWCA) >
1 Macdonnell Rd (green minibus #1A from City Hall) Central Ⓜ Central ☎ 2877 3737, w yhk.com.hk. MAP P.32–33, POCKET MAP D7. Small rooms, but well located near the Botanical Gardens and Lower Peak Tram Terminal. **$1500**

HOTEL LKF >
33 Wyndham St, Lan Kwai Fong, Central Ⓜ Central ☎ 3518 9688, w hotel-lkf.com.hk. MAP P.37, SEE INSET ON POCKET MAP B7. Boutique design, but generously sized rooms, make this a stylish place to stay in Hong Kong's business district. **$2700**

LAN KWAI FONG HOTEL >
3 Kau U Fong Ⓜ Sheung Wan ☎ 3650 0000, w lankwaifonghotel.com.hk. MAP P.32–33, POCKET MAP C5. Not to be confused with *Hotel LKF*, this well-run boutique hotel has rooms furnished with antique-style Chinese furniture and is located near old market streets along the Central–Sheung Wan border. **$1100**

MANDARIN ORIENTAL >
5 Connaught Rd Ⓜ Central ☎ 2522 0111, w mandarinoriental.com. MAP P.32–33, POCKET MAP E6. Considered by many to be Hong Kong's best hotel, with excellent facilities and decor (antique-filled rooms with balconies, and corridors featuring eighteenth-century Chinese textiles), and an ideal location. **$4000**

MOUNT DAVIS YOUTH HOSTEL >
Mount Davis ☎ 2817 5715, w yha .org.hk. MAP P.32–33, POCKET MAP A4. Perched on a mountain above Kennedy Town, this self-catering retreat has superb harbour views. Get the shuttle

Booking accommodation

B ook Hong Kong accommodation directly through hotel websites; for general hotel information visit ⓦ discoverhongkong.com/eng, which has extensive listings and contact details. For Macau, either book direct with accommodation or through a travel agent in Hong Kong.

bus from the Shun Tak Centre (Hong Kong–Macau Ferry Terminal) – phone the hostel for times – or catch a taxi (around $70 plus $10 per item of luggage). **Dorm beds $180, doubles $480**

Wan Chai

BEVERLY > 4/F, 175–191 Lockhart Rd ⓜ Wan Chai ☎ 2507 2026, ⓦ www .bchkhotel.hk. MAP P.50–51, POCKET MAP H7. Rooms are quite spacious and clean, if also lurid. Management are amenable to bargaining, so it's a good deal. **$850**

CONRAD > Pacific Place, 88 Queensway ⓜ Admiralty ☎ 2521 3838, ⓦ conradhotels3.hilton.com. MAP P.50–51, POCKET MAP F7. Modern hotel with well-equipped rooms. Its position on the upper floors of the Pacific Place towers ensures views from all rooms. **$4600**

GRAND HYATT > 1 Harbour Rd ⓜ Wan Chai ☎ 2588 1234, ⓦ hongkong .grand.hyatt.com. MAP P.50–51, POCKET MAP H6. Part of the Convention and Exhibition Centre complex, with harbour views and a luxurious feel. It also has the largest hotel swimming pool in Hong Kong. **$4600**

KING'S > 11/F, 303 Jaffe Rd ⓜ Wan Chai ☎ 3188 2277, ⓦ kingshotelhk.com. MAP P.50–51, POCKET MAP J6. Small, conveniently located low-key hotel; rooms are plain but clean and comfortable and – if booked at vast discount through the website – inexpensive for the island. **$1400**

METRO PARK > 41–49 Hennessy Rd ⓜ Wan Chai ☎ 3604 0000, ⓦ metroparkhotels.com. MAP P.50–51, POCKET MAP H7. Modern, chic place, although the design and layout of the rooms is standard: bed, desk, bathroom, TV and exactly enough floor space to navigate between them. **$2900**

RENAISSANCE HARBOUR VIEW > 1 Harbour Rd ⓜ Wan Chai ☎ 2802 8888, ⓦ renaissancehotels.com/hkghv. MAP P.50–51, POCKET MAP H6. Splendid views and the same expense-account clientele as the adjacent *Grand Hyatt* – whose facilities you get to use – though generally lower rates. **$4000**

Causeway Bay

ALISAN > Flat A, 5/F, Hoito Court, 275 Gloucester Rd ⓜ Causeway Bay ☎ 2838 0762. MAP P.50–51, POCKET MAP L6. Tidy guesthouse with helpful management and a warren of options; rooms are the usual cramped boxes, but all have a/c, TV, shower and phone. **$500**

HOSTEL HK/WANG FAT > 3/F, Paterson Building, 47 Paterson St ⓜ Causeway Bay ☎ 2392 6868, ⓦ hostel.hk. MAP P.50–51, POCKET MAP L6. Basic, bright and clean hostel with a free laundry service and multilingual manager. No sign at street level. **$480**

JETVAN TRAVELLER'S HOUSE > 4/F, 4A Fairview Mansions, 51 Paterson St ⓜ Causeway Bay ☎ 2890 8133, ⓦ jetvan.com. MAP P.50–51, POCKET MAP L6. Popular guesthouse with eight rooms, all with telephone, a/c, TV and bathroom, though some are windowless. **$500**

PARK LANE > 310 Gloucester Rd ⓜ Causeway Bay ☎ 2293 8888, ⓦ parklane.com.hk. MAP P.50–51, POCKET MAP L6. Smart option for business or upmarket travellers, overlooking Victoria Park; well placed for the MTR. **$2300**

Tsim Sha Tsui

BENITO > 7–7B Cameron Rd, Tsim Sha Tsui Ⓜ Tsim Sha Tsui ☎ 3653 0388, Ⓦ hotelbenito.com. MAP P.65, POCKET MAP B17. Bright, clean boutique hotel close to all that matters in Tsim Sha Tsui. Cheaper rooms are small. **$1200.**

BP INTERNATIONAL HOUSE > 8 Austin Rd Ⓜ Jordan ☎ 2376 1111, Ⓦ bpih.com.hk. MAP P.65, POCKET MAP A16. Run by the Scouting organization, this tidy mid-range place has smart doubles facing Kowloon Park, along with triples and quads. **$1300**

GARDEN HOSTEL > Block F4, 3/F, Mirador Mansions, 56–58 Nathan Rd Ⓜ Tsim Sha Tsui ☎ 2311 1183, Ⓦ gardenhostel.com.hk. MAP P.65, POCKET MAP B17. Laidback hostel with a garden terrace. Eight-person dorms are male- or female-only, and rooms are sparklingly clean. **Dorm beds $100, doubles $280**

GERMANY HOSTEL > Block D, 6/F, Chungking Mansions, 36–44 Nathan Rd Ⓜ Tsim Sha Tsui ☎ 9832 4807, Ⓦ germanyhostelhk.com. MAP P.65, POCKET MAP B17. Clean and friendly, with small but welcoming rooms. **Dorm beds $155, doubles $326**

INTERCONTINENTAL > 18 Salisbury Rd Ⓜ Tsim Sha Tsui ☎ 2721 1211, Ⓦ intercontinental.com. MAP P.65, POCKET MAP B18. Rival in quality to the *Peninsula* and the preferred hotel of many business tycoons. **$4000**

LUXE MANOR > 39 Kimberley Rd, Tsim Sha Tsui Ⓜ Tsim Sha Tsui ☎ 3763 8888, Ⓦ theluxemanor.com. MAP P.65, POCKET MAP B16. A boutique option, with stylish themed rooms to appeal or appal. Their *Aspasia* restaurant draws the chic and almost-famous to dine. $1700

MARCO POLO HONGKONG, MARCO POLO GATEWAY, MARCO POLO PRINCE > Harbour City, Canton Rd Ⓜ Tsim Sha Tsui ☎ 2113 1888, Ⓦ marcopolohotels.com. MAP P.65, POCKET MAP A17 & A18. The Harbour City complex houses three different hotels under the same *Marco Polo* umbrella.

They're all fairly fancy, and guests can use any hotel's facilities. Only the *Hongkong* has harbour views; those at the *Prince* overlook Kowloon Park. **$3000**

PENINSULA > Salisbury Rd Ⓜ Tsim Sha Tsui ☎ 2920 2888, Ⓦ peninsula. com. MAP P.65, POCKET MAP B18. Possibly the grandest hotel in Hong Kong, the *Peninsula* has been putting visitors up in unrivalled style since the late 1920s. Its elegant colonial wings have been overshadowed by the new central tower, which provides harbour views. **$3600**

SALISBURY YMCA > 41 Salisbury Rd Ⓜ Tsim Sha Tsui ☎ 2268 7888, Ⓦ ymcahk.org.hk. MAP P.65, POCKET MAP B18. The best-located semi-cheap hotel in town. Facilities include indoor pools, fitness centre and squash court. The a/c doubles with TV and shower are booked up weeks in advance, but there are also 56 beds available in four-bed dorms. **Dorm beds $260, harbour-view doubles $1680**

SEALAND HOUSE > Block D, 8/F, Majestic House, 80 Nathan Rd, Tsim Sha Tsui Ⓜ Tsim Sha Tsui ☎ 2368 9522, Ⓦ sealandhouse.com.hk. MAP P.65, POCKET MAP B17. Located inside a residential block, this is the roomiest and friendliest of the upper-price-range guesthouses, with shared or en-suite facilities. **$500**

STAR GUESTHOUSE > Flat B, 6/F, 21 Cameron Rd Ⓜ Tsim Sha Tsui ☎ 2723 8951, Ⓦ starguesthouse.com.hk. MAP P.65, POCKET MAP B17. Comfortable range of budget singles, doubles and triples in two locations along the road; a bit expensive for what you get though. **$600**

Jordan/Yau Ma Tei

BOOTH LODGE > 7/F, 11 Wing Sing Lane Ⓜ Jordan ☎ 2771 9266, Ⓦ salvationarmy.org.hk. MAP P.76–77, POCKET MAP B14. A Salvation Army hotel close to the Jade and Temple Street markets. Rooms are functional, and there's a restaurant and café. **$1320**

CARITAS BIANCHI LODGE > 4 Cliff Rd Ⓜ Yau Ma Tei ☎ 2388 1111,

Ⓦ www.caritas-chs.org.hk. MAP P.76–77, POCKET MAP B14. Almost next door to *Booth Lodge*, and around twice as big, the a/c rooms in this Roman Catholic-run hotel have bath and TV. **$1200**

KING'S DE NATHAN > 473–473A Nathan Rd, Yau Ma Tei Ⓜ Yau Ma Tei Ⓣ 2780 1281, Ⓦ kingsdenathan .com. MAP P.76–77, POCKET MAP B14. Recently refurbished, with modern furnishings and reasonably sized rooms, this is well located but overpriced for what you get. **$2000**

NATHAN > 378 Nathan Rd Ⓜ Jordan Ⓣ 2388 5141, Ⓦ nathanhotel.com. MAP P.76–77, POCKET MAP B14. Good-value, newly renovated business venue, with fairly spacious rooms featuring broadband internet connections. **$1800**

Mong Kok

DRAGON HOSTEL > Room 707, 7/F, Sincere House, 83 Argyle St Ⓜ Mong Kok Ⓣ 2395 0577, Ⓦ dragonhostel.com. MAP P.76–77, POCKET MAP A11. Guesthouse with helpful management and comparatively large single, double and family rooms that represent a good deal compared with what you'd get in Tsim Sha Tsui. Long-stay rates available. **$400**

ROYAL PLAZA > 193 Prince Edward Rd West Ⓜ Mong Kok Ⓣ 2928 8822, Ⓦ royalplaza.com.hk. MAP P.76–77, POCKET MAP B10. This smart hotel sits on top of Mong Kok MTR station, with an entrance in the Grand Century Place shopping plaza. The 469 rooms come with all the usual amenities but are fairly characterless. There's also a 40m swimming pool, gym, an enormous ballroom and a library. **$2200**

Sham Shui Po

MEI HO HOUSE YOUTH HOSTEL > Block 41, Shek Kip Mei Estate Ⓜ Sham Shui Po Ⓣ 3728 3500, Ⓦ yha.org .hk. MAP P.76–77. Most usefully located of any of Hong Kong's Youth Hostels, featuring the usual institutional collection

of dorms, doubles and a communal kitchen. **Dorm beds $200, doubles $680**

The New Territories

BRADBURY JOCKEY CLUB YOUTH HOSTEL > 66 Tai Mei Tuk Rd, Tai Mei Tuk, Tai Po. Bus #75K from Ⓜ Tai Po Market Ⓣ 2662 5123, Ⓦ yha.org.hk. MAP P.86–87. From the bus terminus, walk towards Plover Cove Reservoir and the hostel is a few minutes ahead on the left. It has two- to eight-bed rooms plus 94 dorm beds, sited at the edge of Plover Cove Country Park. Self-catering facilities only, so bring supplies. **$380**

REGAL RIVERSIDE > Tai Chung Kiu Rd, Sha Tin Ⓜ Sha Tin Wai Ⓣ 2649 7878, Ⓦ regalhotel.com. MAP P.86–87. A comfortable, rather isolated conference-style hotel, about a 15min walk from central Sha Tin. The large rooms are a steal compared to what you'd pay in Tsim Sha Tsui or Central. **$850**

SZE LOK YUEN YOUTH HOSTEL > Tai Mo Shan, Tsuen Wan. Bus #51 from Ⓜ Tsuen Wan, then a 40min walk. Ⓣ 2488 8188, Ⓦ yha.org.hk. MAP P.86–87. This place has camping facilities and 92 dorm beds at the start of trails up Tai Mo Shan's peak (see p.86); self-catering only, so bring supplies. **Dorm beds $115**

Lantau

NGONG PING S.G. DAVIS YOUTH HOSTEL > Ngong Ping. 500m from Po Lin Monastery, signed along the Lantau Trail (see p.97) Ⓣ 2985 5610, Ⓦ yha. org.hk. MAP P.98–99. Camping facilities and 46 beds are available at this basic, self-catering hostel. **$400**

NOVOTEL CITYGATE > 51 Man Tung Rd, Tung Chung Ⓜ Tung Chung Ⓣ 3602 8888, Ⓦ novotel.com. MAP P.98–99. Right next to the Tung Chung MTR and Ngong Ping 360, and close to the airport. Rates are a bargain compared to the downtown areas, and the website often advertises inexpensive last-minute deals. **$1200**

SILVERMINE BEACH RESORT >
Mui Wo ☎ 6810 0111,
Ⓦ silvermineresort.com. MAP P.98–99.
Overlooking the beach at Silvermine Bay,
this is comfortable and great value for
money. There's a swimming pool, gym,
sauna, tennis courts and all the usual
business paraphernalia. **$1200**

Lamma

BALI HOLIDAY RESORT > Yung Shue
Wan ☎ 2982 4504, Ⓦ lammabali
.com. MAP P.103. Apartment block with
spacious rooms, with or without views
and kitchenettes – more modern than
Sunrise (see below), but further back
from the water. **$350–1500**

CONCERTO INN > 28 Hung Shing Ye
Beach, Yung Shue Wan ☎ 2982 1668,
Ⓦ concertoinn.com.hk. MAP P.103.
Lamma's best hotel, offering rooms with
balconies overlooking the beach, satellite
TV, videos and fridges – some have
kitchens. **$920–1400**

KATHMANDU GUESTHOUSE >
Above Bubbles Laundry in Yung Shue
Wan ☎ 2982 0028. MAP P.103. This
hostel-like place has been going forever
and offers dorm beds as well as doubles
at some of the lowest rates on the island.
Dorm beds from $120

SUNRISE HOLIDAY RESORT >
Yung Shue Wan ☎ 2982 0606,
Ⓦ lammaresort.com. MAP P.103. Close
to the ferry, with a range of bright, simple
self-contained flats, some with sea views.
$550–1100

Cheung Chau

B&B > Chung Wan beach ☎ 2986
9990, Ⓦ bbcheungchau.com.hk.
MAP P.104. Pleasant bed-and-breakfast
with a roof terrace for views over the
town and sea. **$650**

BELLA VISTA MIAMI RESORT >
East Bay ☎ 2981 7299,
Ⓦ miamicheungchau.com.hk. MAP P.104.
A huge number of rooms in a residential
block near the east beach. The better
rooms are worth the extra cost. **$550**

WARWICK > East Bay ☎ 2981 0081,
Ⓦ www.warwickhotel.com.hk. MAP
P.104. Overlooking Tung Wan beach,
rooms at this concrete box of a hotel
have balconies, private baths and cable
TV. There's also a terrace café and
pool. **$1450**

Eastern Macau

LISBOA > Av. de Lisboa 2–4
☎ 2888 3888, Ⓦ hotelisboa.com.
MAP P.108–109. A monstrous orange
building with around a thousand rooms,
a bundle of 24hr casinos on several
floors, shops, bars and restaurants, and
an outdoor pool and sauna. **MOP$1020,
royal tower rooms MOP$2020**

MANDARIN ORIENTAL > Av. da
Amizade ☎ 8805 8888,
Ⓦ mandarinoriental.com/macau.
MAP P.108–109. Excellent service
and facilities at this upmarket resort,
tailor-made for families (children's club
and poolside restaurant), corporate
groups (a team-building climbing wall
and trapeze) and the more traditional
Macau visitor (casino and popular bar).
MOP$2400

METROPOLE > Av. da Praia
Grande 493–501 ☎ 8391 1140,
Ⓦ macauctshotel.com. MAP P.108–109.
This well-placed central hotel is just
back from the Praia Grande, and good
value if you're looking for standard rooms
with all the trimmings at a good price.
MOP$1200

NEW NAM PAN > Av. de D. João IV 8
☎ 2848 2842, Ⓦ www.cnmacauhotel
.com. MAP P.108–109. Central, friendly,
modern guesthouse with nine smallish
rooms. Furnishings are a bit plain, and
the beds are hard, but it's clean and good
value for money. **MOP$580**

ROYAL > Estrada da Vitoria 2–4
☎ 2855 2222, Ⓦ hotelroyal.com.mo.
MAP P.108–109. An ageing but good-
value high-rise, close to the Fortaleza
da Guia. A 10min walk from Largo do
Senado, and well equipped, with standard
and deluxe doubles, suites and a pool.
MOP$1300

SANDS > Largo do Monte Carlo 23, Av. da Amizade ☎ 2888 3300, ⓦ sandsmacao.com. MAP P.108–109. The city's first foreign-owned casino offers a choice of luxury suites overlooking the city or bay. MOP$1900

WYNN > Rua Cidade da Sintra ☎ 8986 9966, ⓦ wynnmacau.com. MAP P.108–109, POCKET MAP F12. Macau's most stylish upmarket casino-resort, balancing opulence with taste. MOP$2300

Central and southern Macau

CENTRAL > Av. de Almeida Ribeiro 264 ☎ 2837 3888. MAP P.108–109. One of Macau's oldest hotels, open since 1928, with hundreds of elderly, budget rooms on seven floors, just around the corner from Largo do Senado. Despite being dingy and grubby, the location makes it fair value for money. MOP$260

KO WAH > 3/F, Rua Felicidade 71 ☎ 2893 0755/2837 5599. MAP P.108–109. Budget hotel accessed by lift from the cupboard-sized street lobby, with helpful management. Some rooms are better than others. MOP$450

MAN VA > Rua da Felicidade ☎ 2838 8655, ⓦ manvahotelmacau.com. MAP P.108–109. On a street lined with red wooden doors, this new hotel has clean, modern rooms; bathrooms are spacious and the management helpful, though they don't speak English. Excellent value for money. MOP$450

OLE LONDON > Praça Ponte e Horta 4–6 ☎ 2893 7761, ⓦ olelondonhotel.com. MAP P.108–109. Smart boutique hotel with modern rooms and ADSL available. The cheapest rooms are windowless, so it's best to pay a bit extra to get one overlooking the square. MOP$880

PENSÃO WA FAT > Av. da Praia Grande 622 ☎ 2871 6415. MAP P.108–109. Clean, bright budget hotel; rooms are tiny but have bathrooms. MOP$600

POUSADA DE SÃO TIAGO > Av da República ☎ 2837 8111, ⓦ saotiago.com.mo. MAP P.108–109, POCKET MAP E13. A gloriously preserved seventeenth-century fortress, now an upmarket hotel with swimming pool and terrace bar. MOP$2888, balconied rooms with views around MOP$500 extra

SANVA > Rua da Felicidade 65–67 ⓦ sanvahotel.com. MAP P.108–109. Best budget deal in town, with spotless rooms in an early 1900s building featuring wooden shutters and balconies over Rua Felicidade. MOP$220

SUN SUN > Praça Ponte e Horta 14–16 ☎ 2893 9393, ⓦ bestwestern.com. MAP P.108–109. Smart hotel where the upper floors have a view of the inner harbour. Rooms have TV and bath, and there's plenty of marble and wood in the lobby. MOP$850

Coloane

GRANDE COLOANE RESORT > Estrada de Hác Sá ☎ 2887 1111, ⓦ grandcoloane.com. POCKET MAP G13. Set on Hác Sá's narrow beach, with terraced rooms spread across the hillside. The hotel offers Macau's only 18-hole golf course, two pools and a jacuzzi, with modern, spacious rooms. MOP$1300

POUSADA DE COLOANE > Praia de Cheoc Van ☎ 2888 2143, ⓦ hotelpcoloane.com.mo. POCKET MAP G13. A quirky hotel with 22 rooms, each with its own terrace overlooking the beach. Rooms on the top floor are huge, with sofas, tables and king-sized beds. Apart from its own Portuguese restaurant and a stretch of sand, there's not much else here. MOP$650

VENETIAN > Cotai ☎ 2882 8877, ⓦ venetianmacao.com. POCKET MAP G13. An incredible full-scale replica of St Mark's Square in Venice (including canals with gondolas) fronts a three thousand-room resort, convention centre and casino complex: the convention space here alone is greater than that available in Hong Kong. A sign of the wealth accruing in Macau. From MOP$1400

Arrival

All arrival points in Hong Kong and Macau – airports, train and bus stations, ferry ports and border crossings – are either centrally located or efficiently connected to the downtown areas by public transport.

By air

Hong Kong International Airport

(w hongkongairport.com) is located at Chek Lap Kok, 34km west of Hong Kong Island and just off the northern side of Lantau Island. The Airport Express train or **AEL** (around 6am–1am) runs every eight minutes from here via Kowloon (20min; HK$90, HK$160 return) to Central on Hong Kong Island (24min; HK$100, HK$180 return). Tickets can be bought with cash or credit cards from machines or customer service desks in the arrival halls. **Free shuttle buses** (around 6am–11pm; 2–3 an hour) run from Kowloon and Central AEL stations to selected local hotels; you don't have to be staying at one of them to use the service.

Airport buses (6am–midnight, plus skeleton night service) can take over an hour to get from the airport into town. Buy tickets at customer service desks or on the bus (drivers do not give change). Useful services include the #A11 to Causeway Bay via Central and Wan Chai (every 15–25min; HK$40), and the #A21 to Mong Kok, Yau Ma Tei and Tsim Sha Tsui (every 10min; HK$33).

Taxis from the airport cost HK$300–350 into town, so it's cheaper than taking the AEL for a group of four, though there may be extra charges for luggage ($5 per piece) and for tunnel tolls to Hong Kong Island ($10–15 depending on the tunnel; drivers can legally request you pay the return toll too).

Macau International Airport

(w macau-airport.com) is located at the eastern side of Taipa Island, from where **airport bus** #AP1 (20min; MOP$4.20) meets all flights and runs to the Jetfoil Terminal and *Lisboa* hotel on Avenida da Amizade; a **taxi** into town costs about MOP$40.

Helicopters (HK$/MOP$4450 each way; w skyshuttlehk.com) also shuttle between Hong Kong's Macau Ferry Terminal in Sheung Wan and Macau's Jetfoil Terminal on Avenida da Amizade; see "By ferry" below for public transport available at either terminus.

By ferry

Ferries between Hong Kong and Macau run by Turbojet (w www .turbojet.com.hk) operate from about 7am to midnight, take around an hour and cost from HK$/MOP$164 each way. Ferry tickets can be bought on the day, though it's advisable to book in advance on Friday, Saturday and Sunday. In Hong Kong, you'll arrive at either the **Hong Kong–Macau Ferry Terminal** in the Shun Tak Centre in Sheung Wan, Hong Kong Island (on top of Sheung Wan MTR station), or at the **China Ferry Terminal** on Canton Road, Tsim Sha Tsui, Kowloon (from where Tsim Sha Tsui MTR station is a 10–15min walk). Macau has two ferry terminals, both with connections to Hong Kong and Kowloon. From the **Jetfoil Terminal** on Avenida da Amizade, buses #3, #3A, #10, #28A, #28B and #32 all go past the *Lisboa* hotel, and the #10 or #10A run past Largo do Senado (about 10min), for a flat MOP$3.20. A taxi into town costs around MOP$10. If you arrive at the new **Taipa Terminal**, next to Macau airport, catch bus MT1 to its terminus, outside the *Lisboa*; from here it's a short walk to Largo do Senado.

Macau's **China Ferry Port** is at the Porto Interior on Avenida de Almeida Ribeiro, where daily ferries from Shenzhen dock. Bus #3A from here stops near Largo do Senado, at the *Lisboa* hotel, and at the Jetfoil Terminal (15min).

By train
Trains from China to Hong Kong arrive at Hung Hom Railway Station in Tsim Sha Tsui East (ⓦ mtr.com.hk). You'll also end up here if you cross the border on foot from Shenzhen to Lo Wu or Lok Ma Chau, then catch the East Rail Line (see "Getting around") down through the New Territories. At Hung Hom, signposted walkways lead to a city bus terminal and taxi rank. For Tsim Sha Tsui, stay in the station and catch the MTR one stop south to its terminus at Tsim Sha Tsui East station, which exits into Middle Road. There are no trains to Macau.

By bus
There are buses to downtown Hong Kong from the Chinese border cross-ings and Shenzhen airport (about 30km north); most of these terminate at company depots in Wan Chai, and a few run to Mong Kok in Kowloon. You can book through CTS Hong Kong ⓦ www.ctshk.com.

On foot
Hong Kong has several pedestrian border crossings between Shenzhen in China and the New Territories, but by far the most popular is at Lo Wu (6am–midnight). Formalities are straightforward, and you end up at Lo Wu MTR station, from where trains run south via Tai Po, Sha Tin and Mong Kok to Hung Hom rail station in Kowloon in forty minutes (see "By train" above for onward connections). In Macau, walk across the border via the customs complex (7am–midnight) and catch taxis or

buses to your destination; buses #10 and #3 run down Avenida de Almeida Ribeiro to the centre.

Getting around

Hong Kong has an excellent integrated public transport system. Underground and overground trains, trams, buses and ferries connect almost every part of the territory, and are cheap and simple to use. Macau's public transport is restricted to efficient buses and taxis. Hong Kong tour operators also offer easy ways of day-tripping to Macau and seeing the highlights.

The MTR (Mass Transit Railway)
Hong Kong's speedy **MTR** (daily 6am–1am; trains every few min; ⓦ mtr.com.hk) comprises a handful of lines connecting the north shore of Hong Kong Island with Kowloon, along with the Lantau line, Airport Express Line (AEL), and East Rail and West Rail lines into the New Territories. Maps are colour-coded and bilingual, and **tickets** cost between HK$4 and HK$50 one-way. Ticket machines are on the station concourse – some don't give change and some only take coins. The MTR gets extremely crowded during **rush hour** (8–9.30am & 5.30–7pm).

Light Rail (LR)
Hong Kong's **Light Rail** (ⓦ mtr.com. hk) is an electric, tram-like network linking the western New Territory towns. The only time visitors are likely to use it is to reach the Hong Kong Wetland Park at Tin Shui Wai. Fares cost between HK$4.50 and HK$6.80 per journey.

Buses

Hong Kong's buses (daily 6am–midnight; skeleton night bus service after midnight; ⓦ nwstbus.com.hk) cover just about every corner of the SAR. Each bus is marked with the destination in English and a number, along with a letter: "M" means that it links with an MTR station; "R" buses only run on Sundays and public holidays; and "X" buses are express services with limited stops. **Fares** cost between HK$2.70 and HK$48 per trip – the amount is posted at bus stops and on the buses as you get on. Put the exact fare into the box by the driver; no change is given.

Macau's buses (daily 7am–11pm; a few stop running earlier) operate on circular routes. **Fares** are MOP$3.20 for city routes, MOP$4.20 for Taipa and the airport, and MOP$5 for Coloane ($6.40 to Hác Sá). Pay the driver the exact fare as you get on. The **main terminals** and bus stops are outside the Jetfoil Terminal, in front of the *Lisboa* hotel, near the Maritime Museum and A-Ma Temple, and along Avenida de Almeida Ribeiro.

Trams

Double-decker **trams** (daily 6am–midnight) rattle along the north shore of Hong Kong Island, linking Western, Central, Wan Chai and Causeway Bay; some detour around Happy Valley Racecourse. You alight at the back and pay the flat HK$2.30 **fare** as you exit from the front. Destinations are marked on the front in English.

Ferries

Hong Kong's **cross-harbour ferries** (daily 6/7am until 7–11pm, depending on the service; every few min; ⓦstarferry.com.hk) link north-shore Hong Kong Island with Kowloon – they are suspended, though, in bad weather. The most famous service is the Star Ferry (see p.30); please note that the Star Ferry is not a vessel, but a service – there are several different vessels, named *Morning Star, Evening Star* etc, between Central and Tsim Sha Tsui, though there is another service between between Wan Chai and Tsim Sha Tsui.

Inter-island ferries leave from the Outlying Islands Ferry Piers in front of the IFC2 tower in Central – see island accounts on pp.99, 102 & 105 for details. For Hong Kong–Macau ferries, see "Arrival" on p.132.

Taxis

Hong Kong's taxis are relatively cheap: HK$22 for the first 2km, then HK$1.60 per 200m, though there might be surcharges for carrying luggage and using the cross-harbour tunnels. Cabs are colour-coded for region: red on Hong Kong Island and in Kowloon; green in the New Territories; and blue on Lantau. Cabs for hire display a red flag in the windscreen and an illuminated "Taxi" sign on the roof. Make sure the driver turns the meter

Octopus Cards

For heavy public transport use in Hong Kong, buy an **Octopus Card** (ⓦ www.octopus.com.hk), a rechargeable ticket available from train ticket offices for travel on the MTR, the Airport Express (AEL), Light Rail, trams, most buses, most ferries and minibuses. The card costs an initial HK$150, comprising HK$100 usable value and HK$50 deposit. When it runs out you add credit at machines in rail stations or over the counter at any 7-Eleven store. To use, scan them over sensors at the ticket gates.

on when you get in (though rip-offs are rare). Don't expect drivers to speak English, apart from the names of hotels and streets. If you get stuck, gesture to the driver to radio his control centre, and ask them to translate.

Macau's taxis are also inexpensive: MOP$17 for the first 1.6km, then MOP$2 for every 230m, plus MOP$3 for each piece of luggage. There's also a MOP$2 surcharge between Taipa and Coloane, and a MOP$5 surcharge for airport pick-ups.

Tours

Operators running **English-language tours** in Hong Kong include the Hong Kong Tourist Board (⊚discoverhongkong.com), Splendid Tours (⊚splendid.hk) and Gray Line Tours (⊚hongkong-tour.com). Between them, they arrange half- or full-day coach tours of Hong Kong Island and Kowloon (including sites such as Man Mo Temple, The Peak, Temple Street Night Market, Aberdeen harbour and Stanley Market) from HK$620; a half-day run around Lantau's main sights (HK$670); and ever-popular horseracing tours, which get you into the swanky members' enclosure for a buffet dinner and some racing tips (race days only, dress and minimum age rules apply; from HK$1080 depending on the event). Sunset harbour cruises with a seafood meal are HK$330, and they also offer a full-day tour to Macau (HK$1120).

The HKTB also offers several free short **classes** in tai chi, feng shui, Chinese tea appreciation and even Cantonese opera – book with them at least a day in advance (☎ 2508 1234 for more information).

For a foodie experience to remember, try the Urban Discovery (⊚hongkongfoodietours.com) **food walk**, where you spend an evening sampling local street food and snacks in Sham Shui Po's backstreets.

Directory A-Z

Addresses

Addresses in Hong Kong are easy to read but there is occasional confusion with street level, which is "Ground Floor" (here written G/F) in English, but "First Floor" (1/F) in Chinese. In Macau, lengthy street names are often abbreviated, so that "Avenida do Infante Dom Henrique" becomes "Av do Infante D Henrique".

Cinema

Hong Kong is considered to have the third largest film industry in the world – even if it is threatened with being upstaged by mainland China – an extraordinary feat considering the population is just seven million. Locally made products include police thrillers, kung fu epics, romances and comedies. Cinemas in Hong Kong are mostly multi-screen complexes run by MCL (⊚mclcinema.com), UA (⊚uacinemas.com.hk) and Golden Harvest (⊚goldenharvest.com), and show a mix of international blockbusters (usually screened in the original language, with Chinese subtitles) alongside Chinese-language releases from China, Hong Kong and Tawain.

Crime

Hong Kong and Macau are orderly, community-focused and relatively safe places for visitors. Lock valuables inside bags in hotel rooms, watch out for pickpockets on crowded public transport, and don't wander the backstreets at night, and you should be fine. Hong Kong's Police Headquarters are at Arsenal Street, Wan Chai (☎3661 1612); Macau's are near the tourist information centre on Avenida Sidonio Pais (☎2857 3333).

DIRECTORY A-Z

Electricity

Mains power in Hong Kong and Macau is 220–240V. Hong Kong uses plugs with three square pins (as in the UK); Macau uses both these and plugs with two round pins (as in Europe, China and the US). You can buy adaptors at street markets, shops on the ground floor of Chungking Mansions, or many other places for HK$5–10.

Embassies and consulates

Australia, 23/F, Harbour Centre, 25 Harbour Rd, Wan Chai ☎ 2827 8881; **Canada**, 5/F, 3 Exchange Square, Central ☎ 3719 4700; **China**, 7/F, Lower Block, China Resources Building, 26 Harbour Rd, Wan Chai ☎ 3413 2424; **India**, 16/F, United Centre, 95 Queensway, Admiralty ☎ 3970 9900; **Ireland**, 20/F, 33 De Voeux Rd, Central ☎ 2535 0700; **Japan**, 46/F, One Exchange Square, Central ☎ 2522 1184; **Korea**, 5/F, Far East Finance Centre, 16 Harcourt Rd, Central ☎ 2529 4141; **Malaysia**, 24/F, Malaysia Building, 50 Gloucester Rd, Wan Chai ☎ 2821 0800; **New Zealand**, 6501 Central Plaza, 18 Harbour Rd, Wan Chai ☎ 2525 5044; **Philippines**, 14/F, United Centre, 95 Queensway, Admiralty ☎ 2823 8501; **Singapore**, 901–2 Tower 1, Admiralty Centre, Admiralty ☎ 2527 2212; **South Africa**, 19/F, Great Eagle Centre, 23 Harbour Rd, Wan Chai ☎ 3926 4300; **Thailand**, 8/F, Fairmont House, 8 Cotton Tree Drive, Central ☎ 2521 6481; **UK**, 1 Supreme Court Rd, Admiralty ☎ 2901 3000; **US**, 26 Garden Rd, Central ☎ 2523 9011; **Vietnam**, 15/F, Great Smart Tower, 230 Wan Chai Rd, Wan Chai ☎ 2591 4510.

Gay and lesbian travellers

Macau has no gay or lesbian scene at all, and Hong Kong's is low-key considering the number of people here. *Dimsum* (🌐 dimsum-hk.com) is Hong Kong's gay lifestyle magazine, heavy on articles, lighter on listings and reviews; these are better covered in the "Queer HK" section of *Time Out Hong Kong* (🌐 timeout.com.hk).

Health

GPs in Hong Kong charge around HK$570 a consultation; ask at your accommodation for the closest one. Hong Kong's government hospitals charge non-residents around HK$3100 a day (with HK$19,000 deposit), though casualty visits are free. They include Princess Margaret Hospital, 2–10 Lai King Hill Rd, Lai Chi Kok, Kowloon ☎ 2990 1111; Queen Elizabeth Hospital, 30 Gascoigne Rd, Kowloon ☎ 3506 8888; and Queen Mary Hospital, Pok Fu Lam Rd, Hong Kong Island ☎ 2855 3838. Private hospitals are more expensive, but the standard of care is higher: Hong Kong Baptist Hospital, 222 Waterloo Rd, Kowloon Tong ☎ 2339 8888; Canossa Hospital, 1 Old Peak Rd, Hong Kong Island ☎ 2522 2181; Matilda Hospital, Suite 502, 39 Queen's Rd, Central ☎ 2537 8500.

Dentists are best contacted via the Hong Kong Dental Association (🌐 hkda.org). Treatment is expensive.

In Macau, 24hr medical emergencies are dealt with at the S. Januário Hospital (government), Estrada do Visconde de S. Januário ☎ 2831 3731, or the Kiang Wu Hospital (private), Estrada Coelho do Amara ☎ 2837 1333. For non-urgent cases, head to the Tap Seac Health Centre, between Rua do Campo and Avenida Conselheiro Ferreira de Almeida ☎ 2852 2232.

There are no 24hr pharmacies in Hong Kong or Macau. Watson's and Manning's (daily 9am–7pm or later) are large, ubiquitous Western-style

Emergency numbers

☏ 999 for fire, police or ambulance from a Hong Kong or Macau landline; ☏ 112 from a mobile.

pharmacies stocking toiletries, contact-lens fluid and first-aid items. Some products available over the counter here are prescription-only in Western countries, notably contraceptive pills.

Internet

In Hong Kong, free wifi internet is available at some accommodation, many cafés (for paying customers) and the Central Library, south of Victoria Park, Causeway Bay (Mon, Tues & Thurs–Sun 10am–9pm, Wed 1–9pm). There are also several netbars in the lower floors of Chung-king Mansions, Nathan Rd, Tsim Sha Tsui. In Macau, the tourist office in Largo do Senado has a handful of free terminals, though you may have to queue to use them.

Laundry

Most accommodation offers (expensive) laundry services. Otherwise, there are laundries in almost every Hong Kong back street, charging by the weight of your washing – around HK$30 for a full bag – and taking a couple of hours.

Left luggage

Accommodation can often store luggage, but might have poor security and charge heavily too. Hong Kong has storage lockers at the airport, Airport Express stations, the China–Hong Kong Ferry Terminal (Kowloon), Hung Hom train station (Kowloon) and the Shun Tak Centre (Sheung Wan); in Macau, head to the Jetfoil Terminal. Expect to pay around HK$/MOP$90 per day.

Lost property

Contact the police or, in Hong Kong, offices at Admiralty Station, Tai Wai Station and Siu Hong Station (daily 8am–8pm; ☏ 2861 0020) for things left on trains; or call ☏ 1872920 for items left in taxis.

Massage

Golden Rock Acupressure and Massage Centre of the Blind (8/F, Golden Swan Building, 438 Hennessy Rd, Causeway Bay) and Charlie's Acupressure and Massage Centre of the Blind (Room 1103, Chung Sheung Building, 9–10 Queen Victoria St, Central ☏ acupressuremassage.hk) charge $250 for the first hour, then $100 per thirty minutes to have your body pulled apart by a blind masseur.

A recommended foot masseur is Hong Wai, 7/F, Chung Fung Commercial Building, 12 Canton Rd, Tsim Sha Tsui, who charges $100 for a half-hour reflexology session, or $150 with a shoulder massage included.

Money

Hong Kong dollars (HK$) come in HK$20, 50, 100, 500 and 1000 notes, and 10c, 20c, 50c, HK$1, 2, 5 and 10 coins. Many businesses won't accept HK$1000 bills. Macau uses the pataca (MOP$), made up of 100 avos. Notes come in denominations of MOP$10, 20, 50, 100, 500 and 1000, and coins come as 10, 20 and 50 avos, and MOP$1, 2, 5 and 10.

The pataca is worth three percent less than the Hong Kong dollar, and you can use Hong Kong dollars throughout Macau on a one-for-one basis. You can't use patacas in Hong Kong, however.

Both Hong Kong and Macau have an abundance of banks (Mon–Fri 9am–5pm, Sat 9am–noon) with 24hr ATMs accepting all major foreign credit and debit cards

137

scattered through their downtown areas. Travellers' cheques can be cashed at banks (beware of high transaction fees), or private moneychangers, where you want to watch out for poor exchange rates. Credit cards are useful for high-end purchases but might attract a service charge, and many ordinary businesses (including cheaper restaurants and accommodation) accept cash only.

Opening hours and public holidays

Hong Kong's office hours are Monday to Friday 9am to 5pm, and Saturday 9am to 1pm; shops open daily 10am to 7pm or later in tourist areas; and post offices open Monday to Friday 9.30am to 5pm, Saturday 9.30am to 1pm. Museums often close one day a week. Temples have no set hours, opening daily from early morning to early evening; produce markets tend to kick off at dawn (when they're busiest) and peter out during the afternoon, though speciality markets (such as Temple Street Night Market) have varying opening times.

In Macau, government and official offices open Monday to Friday 8.30/9am to 1pm and 3 to 5/5.30pm, Saturday 8.30/9am to 1pm. Shops and businesses are usually open throughout the day and have slightly longer hours.

On **public holidays** and on some religious festivals most shops and all government offices in both Hong Kong and Macau are closed. For a list of public holidays visit ⓦ www.gov .hk/en/about/abouthk/holiday. See p.140 for details of festivals.

Phones

Local calls from private phones are free in Hong Kong and Macau. For international calls, it's cheapest to buy a discount phone card, where you dial an access number, enter a PIN supplied with the card, then dial the overseas number; costs to the UK, US or Australia are just a dollar or two per minute. Different cards give discounts for specific regions only, so you might have to shop around – Worldwide House in Central and Chungking Mansions in Tsim Sha Tsui (both in Hong Kong) have dozens of places selling them.

The same places also sell inexpensive prepaid local SIM cards for GSM-compatible phones, along with top-up vouchers. To call Macau from Hong Kong use the code +853; use +852 for the reverse.

Post

Hong Kong's post offices are open Monday to Friday between 9.30am and 5pm, and Saturday from 9.30am to 1pm. The GPO is at 2 Connaught Place, Central, Hong Kong Island – poste restante will go here (collection Mon–Sat 8am–6pm); make sure you take your passport along. Airmail letters take around a week to reach Europe or North America.

Macau's GPO (Mon–Fri 9am–6pm, Sat 9am–1pm), where the poste restante mail is sent, is on Largo do Senado; there's also a post office at the Jetfoil Terminal (Mon–Sat 10am–7pm). Delivery times for letters to Europe and North America is the same as from Hong Kong.

Time

Hong Kong and Macau are eight hours ahead of GMT, thirteen hours ahead of New York, sixteen hours ahead of Los Angeles and two hours behind Sydney.

Tipping

In simple restaurants where there's no service charge, it's usual to leave a dollar or two (staff often give change from bills entirely in coins, hoping you'll leave it all). In taxis, make the fare up to the nearest dollar. Porters at upmarket hotels and at the airport require a tip – HK$/MOP$10 is usually ample.

Tourist information

The **Hong Kong Tourist Board** (daily 9am–6pm; ☎ 2508 1234, ⓦ discoverhongkong.com) is well informed about restaurants, accommodation, sights, tours and activities, as well as transport schedules; in addition, they organize free courses on tai chi, Cantonese opera, tea appreciation, pearl grading and more, for which you need to sign up a day in advance. Their downtown offices (daily 8am–8pm) are in the Star Ferry Terminal in Tsim Sha Tsui; and in an old railway carriage outside the Peak Mall, on The Peak.

The **Macau Government Tourist Office** (ⓦ macautourism .gov.mo) offers a limited range of brochures and advice. The main offices are at the Jetfoil Terminal (daily 9am–10pm), and in the centre of Macau at Largo do Senado 9 (daily 9am–6pm). At their Hong Kong office (Macau Ferry Terminal, Shun Tak Tower, Connaught Rd, Central; daily 9am–1pm & 2–6pm; ☎ 2857 2287) you can usually get discounted rates for mid-range hotels prior to departure.

Travellers with disabilities

Hong Kong is reasonably accessible for travellers with disabilities. The Hong Kong Tourist Board's website includes an Accessible Hong Kong page (ⓦ discoverhongkong.com) with links to Hong Kong websites for disabled travellers.

Macau is far less easy to negotiate for physically disabled travellers. The streets are older, narrower, rougher and steeper, and it lacks the overhead ramps and wide, modern elevators that make Hong Kong relatively approachable. Contact the Macau Tourist Office (ⓦ macautourism.gov.mo) before you travel for details of accommodation and transport facilities.

Travelling with children

The Chinese are very child-friendly people as a rule, and make a lot of fuss over both their own offspring and other people's. In addition, both Hong Kong and Macau have abundant attractions – Ocean Park, Disneyland, Hong Kong Wetland Park, Kadoorie Farm, plus a host of museums, temples, festivals, food, shopping and tours – to keep the little ones entertained, many with reduced entry prices for children or families. There are also plenty of supermarkets and chemists with English-speaking staff, where it's possible to find familiar brands of formula, nappies and child medicines.

Some restaurants – most usually Western ones – have child menus, while others might allow you to order half portions; having children in tow, especially young ones, might also secure you half-decent table service. Many of the better hotels offer child-minding services, and public washrooms in urban shopping malls often have changing facilities. Don't breast-feed in public. Things to guard against are the exhausting tropical heat and humidity, poor hygiene, the bustling crowds and constant noise – though frankly these seem to stress out parents more than their children.

Festivals and events

Chinese traditional festival dates are fixed by the lunar calendar, which follows the phases of the moon and is therefore out of step with the Western calendar. We've indicated the likely months in which the following festivals will occur; check with the Hong Kong or Macau tourist offices for specific dates.

CHINESE NEW YEAR (SPRING FESTIVAL)

January/February
Celebrated for the first two weeks of the first month of the lunar calendar. Red and gold decorations, flower markets, lion and dragon dances, and colossal firework displays in both Hong Kong and Macau set the tone. The best public spot to see Hong Kong's harbourside fireworks is at the bottom end of Nathan Road in Tsim Sha Tsui; in Macau it's by the lake on Avenida da Praia Grande – check local papers or tourist office websites for dates. Temples are packed out, too, and families get together to celebrate and eat special "lucky" New Year foods, such as noodles (for long life), fish (because the Chinese word sounds the same as that for "surplus") and crescent dumplings (symbolizing wealth).

YUEN SIU (SPRING LANTERN FESTIVAL)

January/February
Marks the last day of the Chinese New Year (the fifteenth day of the first moon). Brightly coloured paper lanterns symbolizing the moon are hung in parks, shops, temples and houses. There's a second lantern festival in September; see "Mid-Autumn Festival" opposite. Good places to see elaborate arrangements are Victoria and Kowloon parks in Hong Kong, and on the steps of São Paulo in Macau.

CHING MING

April
At the beginning of the third moon, this is also known as "Grave-sweeping day". Families head to old cemeteries up in the hills to burn incense and paper cars, houses, "hell" money and even food at ancestral graves, while prayers are said for the departed souls and blessings sought for the latest generations of the family.

TIN HAU/A-MA FESTIVAL

April/May
Festival to honour the protective goddess of the sea (known as Tin Hau in Hong Kong and as A-Ma in Macau), held on the 23rd day of the third lunar month. Fishing boats are colourfully decorated with flags, streamers and pennants, as fishermen and others who follow the goddess gather at Tin Hau temples (especially at Clearwater Bay) to ask for luck and to offer food, fruit and pink dumplings.

TAM KUNG FESTIVAL

April/May
Honours another patron saint of fishermen on the eighth day of the fourth lunar month, at the temple in Shau Kei Wan on Hong Kong Island.

TAI CHIU (CHEUNG CHAU BUN) FESTIVAL

April/May
A week-long extravaganza on Cheung Chau Island, with dances, operas, martial arts shows, parades and

towers of steamed buns, held to pacify the ghosts of those killed in former times by Cheung Chau's pirates. In deference to the religious nature of the event, no meat is served on the island during this time. The focus is Cheung Chau's Pak Tai Temple, and highlights are the afternoon "floating children" parade on the fifth day, and the scaling of the immense bun tower the following midnight by teams who compete to grab the most buns.

BUDDHA'S BIRTHDAY

May
A low-key celebration when Buddha's statue is taken out of the various Buddhist monasteries and cleaned in scented water. Lantau's Po Lin monastery and the Ten Thousand Buddhas monastery at Sha Tin are the main venues.

TUEN NG (DRAGON BOAT) FESTIVAL

June
Commemorates statesman and poet Chu Yuen, who drowned himself in protest against a corrupt third-century BC government. Teams race in long, narrow boats with dragon-headed prows, and special packets of steamed rice are eaten. Venues include Tai Po, Aberdeen, Tai O on Lantau and Sha Tin.

BIRTHDAY OF LU PAN

July
Banquets are held in honour of this sixth-century BC master carpenter, now patron of builders, on the thirteenth day of the sixth lunar month.

MAIDENS' FESTIVAL

August
Observed on the seventh day of the seventh lunar month by young girls and lovers who burn incense and paper and leave offerings of fruit and flowers. The festival is observed all over Hong Kong, but Lovers Rock in Wan Chai and Amah Rock in the New Territories are particularly popular places of pilgrimage.

YUE LAN FESTIVAL

August
Held on the fifteenth day of the seventh lunar month, when people burn more paper models of food, cars, houses, money and furniture to deflect bad luck and appease "hungry ghosts", said to be set free from hell for the day.

MID-AUTUMN FESTIVAL

September
Also called the Moon Cake Festival after the sweet cakes eaten at this time, and held on the fifteenth day of the eighth lunar month, this festival commemorates a fourteenth-century revolt against the Mongols. Varieties of moon cake (yuek beng) are stacked up in bakeries for the occasion, and there's a big lantern festival in Victoria Park, plus a fire-dragon dance in Tai Hang, on Hong Kong Island.

BIRTHDAY OF CONFUCIUS

September
Low-key religious ceremonies are held at the Confucius Temple in Causeway Bay to mark the birthday of the Chinese thinker and philosopher.

CHEUNG YEUNG FESTIVAL

October
Festival held on the ninth day of the ninth lunar month, when people climb hills in memory of a Han Dynasty man who took his family into the mountains to avoid a natural disaster.

Chronology

4000 BC > Hong Kong and Macau area inhabited by fishermen and farmers.

1279 AD > Fleeing invading Mongol armies, China's last Song emperor dies during a naval battle off Hong Kong.

1368–1660 > The Ming dynasty sees the first substantial settlement of Hong Kong and Macau by Han Chinese (China's dominant ethnic group).

1513–1612 > The Portuguese explore the Pearl River Delta and are allowed by the Chinese government to settle the Macau peninsula as a hub for their expanding trade with Japan and Southeast Asia. The town takes shape in the early seventeenth century, when Jesuits fund the construction of the massive São Paulo cathedral; forts are added from 1612 to repel the Dutch, who are attempting to muscle in on regional trade.

1639 > Dutch intrigues get the Portuguese expelled from Japan; their trading network in Southeast Asia begins to unravel and Macau's fortunes go into a decline.

1750 > The British are allowed to establish trading houses on the southern Chinese mainland at Guangzhou (Canton) city, ending all serious Portuguese influence in the area. The trade is entirely one-sided, however: the British buy Chinese tea and porcelain, but the Chinese find nothing of interest in the range of British products on offer.

c1790–1830 > The British begin to import Indian opium into China. Addiction and demand soar, reversing the flow of money in Britain's favour to the tune of eight million silver pieces a year.

1839 > Chinese authorities attempt to stem the drastic depletion of the country's financial reserves and end the opium trade by blockading British warehouses in Canton, confiscating twenty thousand chests of the drug and publicly destroying them.

1840–42 > The First Opium War. Infuriated by China's actions, Britain sends gunboats to shell cities along the Chinese coast. Britain takes Hong Kong Island in 1841, and the Treaty of Nanking in 1842 concludes the war by allowing the British to establish trading enclaves in Chinese cities.

1846–47 > Taipa is annexed by Macau's Portuguese governor, who also legalizes gambling to increase revenue.

1856–60 > The Second Opium War. British resume gunboat diplomacy to demand greater trading rights in China, and are ceded the Kowloon Peninsula at the Convention of Peking.

1860–80 > Uprisings in China against the failing Qing Dynasty see 150,000 refugees fleeing into Hong Kong. The settlement expands to become a financial and trading centre, with its focus along the north shore of Hong Kong Island.

1887 > China cedes sovereignty of Macau to Portugal.

1898 > The New Territories are leased to Britain for 99 years.

1907 > Britain ends the Chinese opium trade.

1920–41 > Shanghai's rising importance to international trade with China sees Hong Kong's fortunes wobble; from 1933, refugees pour into Hong Kong and Macau as Japan invades China.

1941–45 > The Japanese occupy Hong Kong for most of World War II; following Japanese surrender, the British resume control.

1949–1960s > The Communists seize power in mainland China and more refugees flood in. Hong Kong's population reaches 2.5 million, necessitating the first government housing projects to replace "squatter settlements". The problem intensifies after the Cultural Revolution begins in China in 1964, and the mainland degenerates into near anarchy.

1973–80 > Tuen Mun, Hong Kong's first New Town, opens. The Cultural Revolution fizzles out, and trade with China increases.

1984 > Sino-British Joint Declaration signed, agreeing to hand back Hong Kong after the New Territories lease expires. Hong Kong is to keep its capitalist system for fifty years as a Special Administrative Region (SAR) of China under a "One Country, Two Systems" model.

1985–97 > Hong Kong's economy booms, and competitive architecture blossoms along Hong Kong Island's north shore. The 1989 Tiananmen Square massacre in Beijing causes concern over whether China will be similarly brutal with any post-handover dissent in Hong Kong.

1987 > Portugal and China agree on the return of Macau in 1999 as a SAR.

1997 > Hong Kong is handed back to China; shipping magnate Tung Chee-hwa becomes the SAR's first Chief Executive. The handover is peaceful, but the Asian financial crisis begins a few days later, causing recession and soaring unemployment.

1999–2002 > Macau is returned to China. Local casino monopoly is ended, causing a foreign-funded boom in casino construction.

2003 > SARS (Severe Acute Respiratory Syndrome) kills 299 in Hong Kong; tourist industry crashes.

2005 > Tung Chee-hwa resigns and is replaced by civil servant Donald Tsang. Tsang proves to be a neutral character, keen to build ties with China and establish economic stability in the SAR. He is re-elected for a full term in 2007.

2008–15 > Both Hong Kong and Macau shake off the 2008 global crash, and democratic factions in Hong Kong win 23 of the 30 electable LEGCO seats, giving weight to their campaign for universal suffrage. However, mass demonstrations in 2014 against Chinese government involvement in the election process sees the campaign stall. Meanwhile, an anti-corruption drive in China causes a significant slowdown in Macau's casino economy in 2015.

Language

The primary language in both Hong Kong and Macau is **Cantonese**, a southern Chinese dialect. Cantonese is tonal, so the specific tone with which a word is spoken affects its meaning; mispronounce the tone, and it's like mispronouncing a vowel in English – anything from the wrong meaning to gibberish (for instance, "tall" coming out as "tell", "till", "toll" or "tull"). Cantonese has nine tones, so the opportunities for error are substantial, though context often makes clear what you are trying to say.

Chinese characters embody meanings rather than pronunciation, like written numerals do in the West: the symbol "2" means the same thing in England, Spain and Finland, irrespective of local pronunciation. There are over ten thousand Chinese characters, although you only need around 2500 to read a newspaper. While this is beyond the scope of a short stay, you might learn enough to get the gist of dishes on a menu.

English is widely understood in Hong Kong, though in the countryside speakers can be thin on the ground; all road signs, bus and train timetables, etc are written in both Chinese and English. **Portuguese**, officially Macau's second language, is little used except on signs and restaurant menus.

Using language in Hong Kong and Macau

Included below are lists of the sights covered in this book, some useful words and a menu reader, all with the corresponding Chinese characters. Cantonese pronunciation is not given, as the system for indicating tones requires prior knowledge of the language. A Portuguese menu reader and some useful words for Macau are also included.

Hong Kong sightseeing
PLACES

香港仔	Aberdeen
金鐘	Admiralty
鴨脷洲	Ap Lei Chau
新娘潭	Bride's Pool
銅鑼灣	Causeway Bay
中環	Central
長洲	Cheung Chau
長沙	Cheung Sha
清水灣	Clearwater Bay
鑽石山	Diamond Hill
愉景灣	Discovery Bay
龍脊	Dragon's Back
分流	Fan Lau
跑馬地	Happy Valley
萬宜水庫	High Island Reservoir
香港	Hong Kong
香港島	Hong Kong Island
佐敦	Jordan
錦田	Kam Tin
九龍	Kowloon
南丫島	Lamma Island
蘭桂坊	Lan Kwai Fong
大嶼山	Lantau Island
鳳凰山	Lantau Peak
鯉魚門	Lei Yue Mun
旺角	Mong Kok
梅窩	Mui Wo
新界	New Territories
海運大廈	Ocean Terminal
北潭坳	Pak Tam Au
北潭涌	Pak Tam Chung
船灣郊野公園	Plover Cove Country Park
貝澳	Pui O
淺水灣	Repulse Bay
西貢	Sai Kung
西灣亭	Sai Wan Ting
深水埗	Sham Shui Po
沙田	Sha Tin
沙田坳	Sha Tin Pass
筲箕灣	Shau Kei Wan
石澳	Shek O
上水	Sheung Shui
上環	Sheung Wan
城門郊野公園	Shing Mun Country Park

索罟灣	Sok Kwu Wan
赤柱	Stanley
沙頭角海	Starling Inlet
大浪灣	Tai Long Wan
大尾督	Tai Mei Tuk
大帽山	Tai Mo Shan
大澳	Tai O
大埔	Tai Po
大埔墟	Tai Po Market
天水圍	Tin Shui Wai
尖沙咀	Tsim Sha Tsui
東涌	Tung Chung
維多利亞港	Victoria Harbour
灣仔	Wan Chai
黃大仙	Wong Tai Sin
油麻地	Yau Ma Tei
榕樹灣	Yung Shue Wan

SIGHTS

星光大道	Avenue of Stars
中國銀行大廈	Bank of China
園圃街雀鳥花園	Bird Market
中環廣場	Central Plaza
長江實業中心	The Centre
車公廟	Che Kung Temple
志蓮淨苑	Chi Lin Nunnery
清水灣鄉村俱樂部	Clearwater Bay Country Club
香港會議展覽中心	Convention and Exhibition Centre
交易廣場	Exchange Square
花墟	Flower Market
金魚街	Goldfish Market
香港禮賓府	Government House
跑馬地墳場	Happy Valley Cemeteries
跑馬地馬場	Happy Valley Racecourse
海港城	Harbour City
香港上海匯豐銀行大廈	Hongkong and Shanghai Bank
香港文化中心	Hong Kong Cultural Centre
香港迪士尼樂園	Hong Kong Disneyland
香港文化博物館	Hong Kong Heritage Museum
香港歷史博物館	Hong Kong History Museum
香港公園	Hong Kong Park
香港鐵路博物館	Hong Kong Railway Museum
香港科學館	Hong Kong Science Museum
香港濕地公園	Hong Kong Wetland Park
洪聖廟	Hung Shing Temple
環球貿易廣場	ICC
國際金融中心二期	IFC2
玉器市場	Jade Market
嘉道理農場	Kadoorie Farm
吉慶圍圍村	Kat Hing Wai Walled Village
九龍公園	Kowloon Park
九龍寨城公園	Kowloon Walled City Park
女人街	Ladies' Market
林村許願樹	Lam Tsuen Wishing Trees
立法會大樓	LEGCO building
李鄭屋漢墓	Lei Chung Uk Han Tomb Museum
力寶中心	Lippo Centre
獅子山（郊野公園）	Lion Rock (Country Park)
香港文華東方酒店	Mandarin Oriental Hotel
文武廟	Man Mo Temple
半山自動扶梯	Mid-Levels Escalator
香港藝術館	Museum of Art
香港海防博物館	Museum of Coastal Defence
茶具文物館	Museum of Teaware
南蓮園池	Nan Lian Gardens
午砲	Noon Day Gun
香港海洋公園	Ocean Park
北帝廟	Pak Tai Temple
八仙嶺郊野公園	Pat Sin Leng Country Park
山頂	The Peak
半島酒店	The Peninsula Hotel
寶蓮寺	Po Lin Monastery
三太子宮	Sam Tai Tze Temple

石壁水塘	Shek Pik Reservoir
上窰民俗文物館	Sheung Yiu Folk Museum
信德中心	Shun Tak Centre
嗇色園	Sik Sik Yuen Temple
香港太空館	Space Museum
皇后像廣場	Statue Square
大埔滘自然護理區	Tai Po Kau Nature Reserve
廟街夜市	Temple Street Night Market
萬佛寺	Ten Thousand Buddhas Monastery
天壇大佛	Tian Tan Big Buddha
時代廣場	Times Square
天后廟	Tin Hau Temple
曾大屋圍村	Tsang Tai Uk Walled Village
維多利亞公園	Victoria Park
西港城	Western Market
香港動植物公園	Zoological and Botanical Gardens

STREETS

界限街	Boundary Street
寶雲道	Bowen Road
廣東道	Canton Road
德輔道	Des Voeux Road
告士打道	Gloucester Road
加連威老街	Granville Road
軒尼詩道	Hennessy Road
荷李活道	Hollywood Road
蘭桂坊	Lan Kwai Fong
利源東/西街	Li Yuen Street (east/west)
駱克道	Lockhart Road
南固臺	Nam Koo Terrace
彌敦道	Nathan Road
砵典乍街	Pottinger Street
皇后大道	Queen's Road
皇后東大道	Queen's Road East
新填地街	Reclamation Street
上海街	Shanghai Street
太原街	Tai Yuen Street

TRANSPORT

巴士站	Bus stop
赤鱲角機場	Hong Kong International Airport
中港碼頭	China Ferry Terminal
輕便鐵路車站	LR station
纜車總站	Lower Peak Tram Terminal
港澳碼頭	Macau Ferry Terminal
地下鐵車站	MTR station
昂坪360	Ngong Ping 360
港外線碼頭	Outlying Islands Ferry Pier
天星碼頭	Star Ferry Pier

Macau Sightseeing

PLACES

媽閣	Barra
路環	Coloane
澳門	Macau
外港	Porto Exterior
內港	Porto Interior
氹仔	Taipa

SIGHTS

媽閣廟	A-Ma Temple
基督教墳場	Cemitério Protestante
竹灣	Cheoc Van
路環市區	Coloane Village
澳門漁人碼頭	Fishermans' Wharf
東望洋山堡壘	Fortaleza da Guia
大炮台	Fortaleza do Monte
松山	Guia Hill
黑沙海灘	Hác Sá Beach
康公廟	Hong Kung Temple
葡京酒店	Lisboa Hotel
盧廉若公園	Jardim Lou Lim Ieoc
白鴿巢賈梅士花園	Jardim Luís de Camões
觀音堂	Kun Iam Temple
議事亭前地	Largo do Senado
議事亭	Leal Senado
蓮峰廟	Lin Fong Temple
連溪廟	Lin Kai Temple
澳門文化中心	Macau Cultural Centre

澳門博物館	Museu de Macau
林則徐博物館	Museu Lin Zexu
海事博物館	Museu Maritimo
北帝廟	Pak Tai Temple
石排灣郊野公園	Parque de Seac Pai Van
主教山教堂	Penha Chapel
關閘	Portas de Cerco
聖地牙哥	Pousada de São Tiago
港局大樓	Quartel dos Mouros
紅街市	Red Market
路環聖方濟各教堂	St Francis Xavier Chapel
仁慈堂大樓	Santa Casa de Misericórdia
聖澳斯定教堂	Santo Agostinho
聖母玫瑰堂	São Domingos
大三巴牌坊	São Paulo
大堂	Sé
氹仔舊城區	Taipa Village
伯多祿五世劇院	Teatro dom Pedro V
三盞燈	Three Lamps District
天后古廟	Tin Hau Temple
威尼斯人度假村	The Venetian

STREETS

友誼大馬路	Avenida da Amizade
民國大馬路	Avenida da Republica
新馬路	Avenida de Almeida Ribeiro
南灣大馬路	Praia Grande
龍嵩正街	Rua Central
福隆新街	Rua da Felicidade
草堆街	Rua das Estalagens
十月初五街	Rua de Cinco de Outubro
河邊新街	Rua do Almirante Sérgio
板樟堂街	Rua Sul do Mercado de São Domingos

TRANSPORT

蛇口碼頭	China Ferry Terminal
港澳碼頭	Jetfoil Terminal
澳門機場	Macau Airport

Useful words
SOME CANTONESE SIGNS

入口	Entrance
出口	Exit
廁所	Toilets
男廁	Gentlemen
女廁	Ladies
營業中	Open
休業	Closed
到達	Arrivals
出發	Departures
休假	Closed for holidays
出故障	Out of order
礦泉水	Drinking/mineral water
請勿吸煙	No Smoking
危險	Danger
關稅	Customs
公共汽車	Bus
渡船	Ferry
火車	Train
飛幾場	Airport
警察	Police
飯店	Restaurant
賓館	Hotel
野營位置	Campsite
海灘	Beach
禁止游泳	No Swimming

SOME PORTUGUESE WORDS

Alfândega	Customs
Avenida	Avenue
Baía	Bay
Beco	Alley
Bilheteira	Ticket office
Calçada	Cobbled street
Correios	Post office
Edifício	Building
Estrada	Road
Farmácia	Pharmacy
Farol	Lighthouse
Fortaleza	Fortress
Hospedaria	Guesthouse
Jardim	Garden
Largo	Square
Lavabos	Toilets
Mercado	Market
Museu	Museum

Pensão	Guesthouse
Ponte	Bridge
Pousada	Inn/Hotel
Praça	Square
Praia	Beach
Rua	Street
Sé	Cathedral
Travessa	Lane
Vila	Guesthouse

Hong Kong menu reader

GENERAL

我食齋	I'm vegetarian
菜單/英文菜單	Menu/English menu
筷子	Chopsticks
刀/叉/匙羹	Knife/fork/spoon
埋單	Bill/cheque

DRINKS

啤酒	Beer
咖啡	Coffee
(礦泉) 水	(Mineral) Water
葡萄酒	Wine
白酒	Spirits
豆漿	Soya milk
茶	Tea
紅茶	Black tea
綠茶	Green tea
鐵觀音茶	"Iron Buddha" tea
香片茶	Jasmine tea
普洱茶	Bo lei tea
苦茶	Medicinal tea
五花茶	Five-flower tea
甘四味茶	Twenty-four flavour tea

STAPLE FOODS

竹筍	Bamboo shoots
芽菜	Bean sprouts
豆角	Beans
牛肉	Beef
牛肉丸	Beef ball
豆豉醬	Black bean sauce
雞	Chicken
辣椒	Chilli
菜心	Chinese greens
蟹	Crab
青瓜	Cucumber
鴨	Duck

鰻魚	Eel
魚	Fish
蒜頭	Garlic
薑	Ginger
鵝	Goose
青椒	Green pepper
羊肉	Lamb
味精	MSG
磨菇	Mushrooms
麵條	Noodles
蠔油	Oyster sauce
白鴿	Pigeon
豬肉	Pork
大蝦	Prawns
蝦丸	Prawn balls
河粉	Rice noodles
白飯	Rice, boiled
鹽	Salt
芝麻油	Sesame oil
湯	Soup
豉油	Soy sauce
魚	Squid
糖	Sugar
豆腐	Tofu/Beancurd
醋	Vinegar
白蘿卜	White radish

COOKING METHODS

焙	Casseroled
沙鍋	Claypot/sandpot
煮	Boiled
炒	Fried
白煮	Poached
烤	Roast
蒸	Steamed
清炒	Stir-fried

MAIN DISHES

叉燒 (飯)	Barbecued pork (on rice)
豆腐湯	Beancurd soup
牛肉丸湯	Beef ball soup
燉鴨素菜	Braised duck with vegetables
客家豆腐	Casseroled beancurd stuffed with pork mince
筍尖嫩玉米炒雞片	Chicken with bamboo shoots and baby corn

Dim sum menu reader

Savouries

Steamed prawn dumplings	蝦餃
Steamed beef ball	山竹牛肉
Steamed spare ribs	排骨
Steamed pork and prawn dumpling	燒賣
Steamed bun stuffed with barbecued pork	叉燒飽
Steamed chicken bun	雞飽
Steamed rice-flour roll stuffed with beef	牛肉腸粉
Steamed rice packet stuffed with chicken, wrapped in a lotus leaf	糯米雞
Deep-fried wonton with sweet and sour sauce	炸雲吞
Congee (rice porridge, flavoured with shredded meat and vegetables)	粥
Spring roll	春卷
Radish cake	蘿蔔糕
Chicken feet	鳳爪
Stuffed green peppers	煎釀青椒
Taro/yam croquette	芋角
Prawn rice roll	蝦腸粉
Shark's fin dumplings*	魚翅餃
Steamed fishballs	鯪魚球
Crispy-fried squid tentacles	炸魷魚鬚
Fried rice-flour ball stuffed with meat	咸水角
Deep-fried beancurd roll with pork/shrimp	鮮竹卷
Crystal-skinned dumpling	潮洲粉果
"Thousand-year" preserved eggs	皮蛋

*named after the shape – they don't contain shark's fin

Sweets

Cold beancurd with syrup	豆腐花
Coconut jelly	椰汁糕
Steamed sponge cake	馬拉糕
Mango pudding	芒果布甸
Sweet lotus-seed paste bun	蓮蓉飽
Egg-custard tart	蛋撻

腰果雞丁	Chicken with cashew nuts	燒肉(飯)	Crisp-skinned pork (on rice)
蠔油芥蘭	Chinese broccoli in oyster sauce	蛋炒飯	Egg fried rice
		魚丸湯	Fish ball soup
沙鍋腊腸飯	Claypot rice with sweet sausage	焙魚	Fish casserole
豉汁焗蟹	Crab with black beans	清蒸魚	Fish steamed with ginger and spring onion

豆腐素菜	Fried beancurd with vegetables
炒豆芽	Fried bean sprouts
檸檬雞	Lemon chicken
羅漢齋	Monks' dish (stir-fry of vegetables and fungi)
湯麵	Noodle soup
蒜頭炒蝦	Prawn with garlic sauce
燒鴨(飯)	Roast duck (on rice)
燒鵝	Roast goose
客家鹽幾	Salt-baked chicken
豆豉青椒炒魚	Squid with green pepper and black beans
豆豉蒸鰻	Steamed eel with black beans
清炒竹筍	Stir-fried bamboo shoots
筍尖炒雞片	Stir-fried chicken and bamboo shoots
糖醋排骨	Sweet and sour spare ribs
雲吞湯	Wonton soup

Macau menu reader

GENERAL

Almoço	Lunch
Comidas	Meals/dishes
Jantar	Dinner
Prato do dia/Menu do dia	Dish/menu of the day

BASICS AND SNACKS

Arroz	Rice
Batatas fritas	French fries
Legumes	Vegetables
Manteiga	Butter
Omeleta	Omelette
Ovos	Eggs
Pimenta	Pepper
Prego	Steak roll
Sal	Salt
Salada mista	Mixed salad
Sandes	Sandwiches

MEAT

Almôndegas	Meatballs
Bife	Steak
Chouriço	Spicy sausage
Coelho	Rabbit
Cordoniz	Quail
Costeleta	Chop, cutlet
Dobrada	Tripe stew
Figado	Liver
Galinha	Chicken
Pombo	Pigeon
Porco	Pork
Salsicha	Sausage

FISH AND SEAFOOD

Amêijoas	Clams
Bacalhau	Dried, salted cod
Camarões	Shrimp
Carangueijo	Crab
Gambas	Prawns
Linguado	Sole
Lulas	Squid
Mexilhões	Mussels
Pescada	Hake
Sardinhas	Sardines

SOUPS

Caldo verde	Green cabbage and potato soup, often served with spicy sausage
Sopa álentejana	Garlic and bread soup with a poached egg
Sopa de mariscos	Shellfish soup
Sopa de peixe	Fish soup

COOKING TERMS

Assado	Roasted
Cozido	Boiled, stewed
Frito	Fried
Grelhado	Grilled
No forno	Baked

SPECIALITIES

Camarões	Huge grilled prawns with chillies and peppers

Cataplana	Seafood with bacon, sausage and peppers
Cozido á Portuguesa	Boiled casserole of mixed meats, rice and vegetables
Galinha á Africana (African chicken)	Chicken baked with peppers and chillies
Galinha á Portuguesa	Chicken baked with eggs, potatoes, onion and saffron in a curry sauce
Feijoada	Rich stew of beans, pork, sausage and vegetables
Pasteis de bacalhau	Cod fishcakes, deep-fried
Porco á álentejana	Pork and clams in a stew
Pudim flán	Creme caramel
Arroz doce	Portuguese rice pudding

DRINKS

Água mineral	Mineral water
Café	Coffee
Chá	Tea
Cerveja	Beer
Sumo de laranja	Orange juice
Vinho tinto	Red wine
Vinho branco	White wine
Vinho do Porto	Port (both red and white)
Vinho verde	young wine, slightly sparkling and refreshing; usually white

Glossary

AEL Airport Express Line, running between Hong Kong Island, Kowloon and HK International Airport at Chek Lap Kok.

A-Ma see "Tin Hau".

Ancestral hall Temple hall where ancestral records and shrines are kept.

BOC Bank of China.

Dim sum Cantonese-style breakfast made up of a selection of small soups, dumplings and special dishes, served with tea. Also known as *yum cha*.

Feng shui The belief that the arrangement of local landscape affects an area or building's "luck".

Gweilo European, foreigner.

Hakka Chinese ethnic group who live in distinctive clan villages.

Handover The formal handing back of Hong Kong by Britain to China in 1997.

HKTB Hong Kong Tourist Board.

HSBC Hongkong and Shanghai Bank.

ICC International Commerce Centre – Hong Kong's tallest building.

IFC2 International Finance Centre, Tower 2.

Kun Iam See "Kwun Yam".

Kwun Yam The Chinese Boddhisattva of Mercy, especially prayed to by women wanting children and safe childbirth.

LEGCO Hong Kong's Legislative Council.

Mainland China, excepting Hong Kong and Macau.

MTR Mass Transit Railway – Hong Kong's urban rail network.

New Territories The area of Hong Kong between Kowloon and the Chinese border.

New Towns Self-contained satellite towns spread across the New Territories, designed to decentralize Hong Kong's urban population.

Pastelaria Macanese sweet/savouries shop specializing in almond biscuits, peanut brittle and roast meats.

SAR Special Administrative Region of China, hence "Hong Kong SAR" and "Macau SAR". Though technically controlled by the Chinese government, SARs enjoy considerably more local autonomy and freedoms than is permitted on the mainland.

SARS Severe Acute Respiratory Syndrome, a virus which killed 299 people in Hong Kong in 2003.

Tin Hau Sea goddess and protector of fishermen; known as A-Ma in Macau.

Triad Organized crime gang, similar to the Mafia.

Yum cha see "dim sum".

PUBLISHING INFORMATION

This third edition published September 2016 by **Rough Guides Ltd**

80 Strand, London WC2R 0RL

11, Community Centre, Panchsheel Park, New Delhi 110017, India

Distributed by Penguin Random House

Penguin Books Ltd, 80 Strand, London WC2R 0RL

Penguin Group (USA) 345 Hudson Street, NY 10014, USA

Penguin Group (Australia) 250 Camberwell Road, Camberwell, Victoria 3124, Australia

Penguin Group (NZ) 67 Apollo Drive, Mairangi Bay, Auckland 1310, New Zealand

Penguin Group (South Africa) Block D, Rosebank Office Park, 181 Jan Smuts Avenue,

Parktown North, Gauteng, South Africa 2193

Rough Guides is represented in Canada by

DK Canada 320 Front Street West, Suite 1400, Toronto, Ontario M5V 3B6

Typeset in Minion and Din to an original design by Henry Iles and Dan May.

Printed and bound in Malaysia

© David Leffman 2016

Maps © Rough Guides

160pp includes index

A catalogue record for this book is available from the British Library

ISBN 978-0-24125-282-6

The publishers and authors have done their best to ensure the accuracy and currency of all the information in **Pocket Rough Guide Hong Kong and Macau**, however, they can accept no responsibility for any loss, injury, or inconvenience sustained by any traveller as a result of information or advice contained in the guide.

1 3 5 7 9 8 6 4 2

MIX
Paper from
responsible sources
FSC™ C018179
www.fsc.org

ROUGH GUIDES CREDITS

Editor: Emma Gibbs

Layout: Ankur Guha

Cartography: Katie Bennett

Picture editor: Phoebe Lowndes

Photographer: Tim Draper

Proofreader: Anita Sach

Managing editor: Andy Turner

Production: Jimmy Lao

Cover photo research: Nicole Newman

Editorial assistant: Freya Godfrey

Senior pre-press designer: Dan May

Publishing director: Georgina Dee

THE AUTHOR

David Leffman first visited Hong Kong in 1985 and seems to have spent most of his life since contributing to books about the Chinese world. He has a degree in photography and studied Mandarin Chinese at SOAS, London and Sichuan University, China. He has also co-authored and edited guidebooks to Australia, China, Indonesia, Hong Kong, Iceland and Malaysia for Rough Guides, Dorling Kindersley and others.

HELP US UPDATE

We've gone to a lot of effort to ensure that the third edition of the **Pocket Rough Guide Hong Kong and Macau** is accurate and up-to-date. However, things change – places get "discovered", opening hours are notoriously fickle, restaurants and rooms raise prices or lower standards. If you feel we've got it wrong or left something out, we'd like to know, and if you can remember the address, the price, the hours, the phone number, so much the better.

Please send your comments with the subject line "**Pocket Rough Guide Hong Kong and Macau Update**" to ✉ mail@roughguides.com. We'll credit all contributions and send a copy of the next edition (or any other Rough Guide if you prefer) for the very best emails.

Find more travel information, connect with fellow travellers and plan your trip on Ⓦ www.roughguides.com

PHOTO CREDITS

All photos © Rough Guides except the following:
(Key: t-top; c-centre; b-bottom; l-left; r-right)

1 Corbis: Jean-Pierre Lescourret
2 AWL Images: Travel Pix Collection
4 Getty Images: Keren Su
5 Getty Images: Esch Collection
6 Alamy Stock Photo: Sean Pavone
8 Alamy Stock Photo: myLAM (c)
9 Alamy Stock Photo: Andrew Linscott (t); FLPA (c); Courtesy of Iain Masterson (b)
11 Axiom: Ian Cumming. Alamy Stock Photo: Prisma Bildagentur
15 Superstock: JTB. Getty Images: Peter Adams
16 Getty Images: Samantha Sin
17 Getty Images: Ed Jones (t); Corbis: Reuters / Tyrone Siu (cl)
21 Alamy Stock Photo: John Warburton (cr); Steve Vidler (cl)
22 Alamy Stock Photo: age footstock / Ian Trower

24 Alamy Stock Photo: Justin Yeung
25 Alamy Stock Photo: Lyndon Giffard (cl)
26 SuperStock: Steve Vidler
36 Alamy Stock Photo: Simon Meaker
42 Alamy Stock Photo: Lyndon Giffard Images
45 Courtesy of Mandarin: Oriental Hong Kong
52 Alamy Stock Photo: World Pictures
53 Alamy Stock Photo: Ian Trower
84 age fotostock: ZoonarJess Yu
85 Getty Images: Michael Siward
103 Alamy Stock Photo: Robert Harrison
121 Alamy Stock Photo: Emma Wood

Front cover and spine: *Neon signs along Nathan Road in Hong Kong at night* **Alamy Stock Photo:** Paul Springett 07
Back cover: *Kowloon Hong Kong night cityscape* **Alamy Stock Photo:** Chris Putnam

Index

Maps are marked in **bold**.